THE MAKING OF
GEMMS
A Guide To Mentoring

By Michelle Easley & Deana Easley

Positive Push Press, LLC
©2008

First printing 2008

This book is a compilation of information obtained from various sources and from the authors' personal experiences. Any slights against people or organizations are unintentional. Every effort has been made to ensure that the accuracy and completeness of the information contained within, the authors assume no responsibility for error, inaccuracies, omissions or inconsistencies.

This publication is intended to provide guidance as it relates to the topics being presented. It is sold with the understanding that the authors and publisher are not herein engaged in rendering legal, or psychological advice. Persons working with minors must abide by the laws governing their states and are encouraged to seek counsel from a professional attorney. Forms included are merely guides. The authors and publisher disclaim any personal liability, directly or indirectly, for advice or information presented within.

ISBN: 978-0-9798358-0-3

ATTENTION EDUCATIONAL INSTITUTIONS, COPRORATIONS, NONPROFIT ORGANIZATIONS, PROFESSIONAL ORGANIZATIONS: Quantity discounts are available on bulk purchases of this book for educational, gift purposes, subscription incentives or fundraising campaigns. Special books or book excerpts can also be created to fit specific needs. For information, please contact Positive Push Press LLC, P.O Box 43811, Atlanta, Georgia 30336 www.positivepushpress.com

Edited by Denise Jones
Cover design by Candace A. Scott
Web design by Kevin & Shauna Easley

This book is dedicated to Madison Nicole Easley,
Ny'Tasha Easley, Amber Easley, and girls around the globe,
GEMMS *in the making: Gifted, Elegant, Magnificent & Motivated Sisters*
and the women who care enough to answer the call to mentor.

Your Shoulder for Your Sister

Things will get hard as they often do.
I know it's difficult girl, but you can make it through.
Life will test and try you; you know what to do,
You do your part and God will too.
Fall on your knees girl, pray night and day
Never give up, because you're on your way!
Keep the faith. Don't turn around.
Listen for the angels singing; what a joyous sound.
Look back and rejoice! You made it through the darkest night.
But don't forget your sister; she needs your help to fight,
to stay the course and stay alive.
She needs your touch to survive.
She needs your words of wisdom, love and care.
She'll be right behind you, if only you will share.
Let your shoulder be her quiet resting place
Tell her of His love, mercy, peace and grace.

–Michelle Easley

CONTENTS

Chapter 4

Chapter 5

INTRODUCTION

"Dear brothers and sisters, if another Christian is overcome by some sin, you who are godly should gently and humbly help that person back onto the right path. And be careful not to fall into the same temptation yourself. Share each other's troubles and problems and in this way obey the law of Christ."

Galatians 6: 1- 2 New Living Translation

"Invest in the human soul. Who knows, it might be a diamond in the rough."
-Mary McLeod Bethune

What is the world coming to? What does our future hold? How can we save these girls? Grim statistics tell us that sexually transmitted diseases among teens are rampant. Unplanned teenage pregnancies are common place. Drop out rates and chemical dependency are at an all time high and a general decline in moral character is clearly evident. The existence of these problems comes as no surprise. All one has to do is watch the evening news to get an even more disturbing picture. Many of our young people, especially our teen girls, live in a state of crisis. Our young ladies are growing up in an environment where disrespect and blatant degradation are the norm, rather than the exception being bombarded with glamorous images of video vixens, set against the backdrop of a sometimes violent hip hop world. Many lack proper guidance and cannot look to home for stability and support. Parents may be ill equipped and overburdened with life's daily pressures and demands. It's not that they don't want to help; they may not know how to help or need help themselves. If we don't make an effort to save our girls, who will?

Could you be that lifesaver? It only takes one caring and committed adult to provide direction and guidance to enable girls to become productive, Christian young women. A smile, a kind word, or an expression of heartfelt concern makes a substantial difference in the life of a girl. Never underestimate your power. One person can change the fate of another. Imagine what several dedicated women might accomplish with just a few hours a week and a small group of girls. Your gatherings will produce significant, positive change. Most young people only need a gentle nudge in the right direction. After all, we are awesome creations of God. Help to inspire a young woman to accomplish incredible goals. You may have a young woman in your midst that will develop a cure for cancer, and AIDS, become the next president of the United States or the diplomat that will broker world peace. This guide is written for you. It will empower you to create a comprehensive, practical program for girls.

This book was born out of a need to reach girls struggling to make it in the sometimes difficult life circumstances of poverty and despair. We, the authors of this book, spent several years working with girls in an urban environment in an organization that we founded: GEMMS: Gifted, Elegant, Magnificent, Motivated Sisters. We discovered that most of the young ladies we dealt with were like diamonds in the rough. They lacked direction in making sensible life decisions. Some were in distress due to troubling situations at home and in school. Many lived in extreme poverty and seldom had the opportunity to see positive, female, role-models. We realized they were stones waiting to be polished to their ultimate brilliance. Our organization furnished the motivation and encouragement that many of the girls needed to reach their full potential.

The goal of this book is to provide guidance on life issues and spiritual challenges by empowering and equipping girls to make healthy, positive choices that glorify God. It is a guide to mentoring girls, tweens, teens and young adults. This book shares the love of God, and promotes spiritual growth and increased self-esteem. It is designed to equip you to work with individuals, small groups or large groups. You may be in a one-on-one mentoring relationship, or you may be working with a group of girls. Whatever the case, the information contained herein will maximize the positive influence you have on girls. This book can be used effectively in churches, retreats, youth conferences, school groups, youth detention centers, group homes, nonprofit and community organizations.

Through role-playing, discussion, journaling, questioning, artistic expression, and real-world learning young women are challenged to explore and grow in new directions. The book is Bible-based, relevant, and thought provoking. The chapters are formatted in the following manner:

GATEWAY – Introduction & Warm up activities

ECHOES – Group activities

MILESTONES – Reflection through journaling

MAGNETS – Parent Activities & handouts (Pearls for Parents)

SANCTUARY – Closing activities & prayer

PRECIOUS JEWEL – SCRIPTURAL REFERENCE

This is a scriptural reference, and a quote. The scripture may be presented by the adult facilitator or read aloud by a participant. It can also be posted in the room. Scriptures are taken from the New International Version of the Bible unless otherwise noted in text. The quote is targeted and thought-provoking; it serves to introduce information presented in each chapter.

GATEWAY

INTRODUCTION
Factual information, research, statistics, and rationale are provided for each topic, including real life scenarios.

MIXERS
Mixers include warm-up activities that will motivate your group and set the tone for the topic being explored.

ECHOES

GROUP ACTIVITIES
Group activities are innovative and creative approaches to dealing with the serious issues presented. These activities are interactive and provide real-world learning.

MILESTONES

WRITING ABOUT THE TOPICS
Writing prompts are provided to encourage personal reflection through journaling. Pages are included at the end of each chapter for you to reproduce and use.

MAGNETS
Magnets are suggested activities and tips to create successful parent mini-workshops. These strategies will enhance the level of parental involvement.

PEARLS FOR PARENTS
Pearls for Parents are handouts which contain helpful suggestions and tips for effective parenting.

SANCTUARY
Sanctuary is a closing prayer or activity that wraps up the session.

Resources, web sites and sample forms are included. At the end of each chapter, you will find reproducible handouts relating to the topics presented. The task before you is not an easy one, but it is necessary. Our prayers are for you and with you. We encourage you to be inspired and stay the course; a young woman's life depends on you. Through God all things are possible. Remember Philippians 4:13; "I can do everything through him who gives me strength."

CHAPTER 1
Getting Started

It's time to get started. How will you get the young ladies to come? Let your own creativity be your guide. Create a flyer (located at the end of the chapter) to post and distribute at schools, churches, apartment complexes, community centers, health centers, laundromats, subdivisions, and libraries, wherever you think the girls may be. Post office, grocery store bulletin boards and local restaurants may be excellent locations as well. You may even wish to use free public service announcements on local radio and television stations.

Once you have assembled a group of volunteers the real work begins.

- Establish your meeting schedule.

- Secure a meeting location. The ideal location to hold your meeting may be a church, school, or community center. Your home can be used if there are no other options available.

- Set up the time and day your group will meet in advance, whether it's once a month or twice a week. It's up to you. Just remember, once your schedule is set it will be critical you remain consistent.

- Create an information sheet for your participants and their parents to include the meeting time, date and location. Don't forget to indicate when the group **will not meet.** Include your contact information, phone and email address.

- Require girls to bring in signed parental permission forms and complete a personal information sheet at the first meeting. (Sample forms can be found at the end of the chapter.)

Organization is the key to success. Purchase a file box or notebook specifically for your group. Make sure you keep all pertinent documents in this location for quick reference later.

Most importantly, have a spirit of jubilant expectation. Open yourself and welcome the opportunity to learn. You'll probably learn more than the girls you will help.

Tips for a successful meeting…

1. Encourage the girls to actually help you create a list of rules. This will make your meetings run more efficiently. Don't just list rules, allow the girls to have input. Hopefully, the list created will reflect the following, if not you may wish to gently steer your list of rules in this direction:

    • Switch cell phone off or to vibrate.

    • No food and beverages allowed in the meeting room.

    • Show respect for self and others.

    • Respect adult leaders.

    • Be willing to listen.

    • Gossiping is not allowed.

    • Inappropriate language is not permissible.

2. Have the following **materials** on hand for your sessions: Bibles, pencils, pens, glue, CD player,favorite gospel/ Christian/ classical/ jazz CD, name tags, markers, colored pencils, crayons, construction paper and pocket folders.

3. Make your meeting room a sacred place. Create a calm and inviting atmosphere. Invite girls to leave the cares of the world on the outside of the room. After they are seated instruct them to breathe deeply, relax and listen to the music.

4. Each session should begin with prayer led by an adult facilitator. After you have met with the girls for a while you may ask them to lead the opening prayer.

5. Have the girls commit to memory the *GEMMS Pledge of Loyalty* to self and God.

THE GEMMS PLEDGE

We are **GEMMS**; Gifted, Elegant, Magnificent, Motivated Sisters
We will honor, love and respect God and ourselves.
We will always be considerate of others.
We strive for excellence in everything we do.
We are beautiful, intelligent, unique, special creations of God.

6. After the pledge the girls will move into discussion and activities. Detailed information on topics and other activities are presented in the subsequent chapters. You may follow this format for each session.

GEMMS

JOIN US
FOR FUN, FELLOWSHIP & FOOD
GIRLS ONLY!!
SUNDAY, 3:00 – 4:00 PM
CHURCH FELLOWSHIP HALL

PARENTAL PERMISSION

Name
Parent or Guardian's Name

Address	Apt. #

City	State	Zip
Phone		
E-mail Address		

School	
	Grade

Media Release: I hereby grant *[insert your group's name here]* _____ permission to use film, or photographs of the above mentioned minor for lawful informational purposes.

Parent or Guardian Signature _____

Parental Permission: I, the legal guardian/parent grant permission for _____ to participate in _____ *[insert your group's name here]* activities. I agree to hold harmless _____ *[insert your group's name here]* from claim(s) of any nature arising from any activity connected with _____ *[insert your group's name here]*.

_____

Parent/Guardian Signature   Date

_____ (girl's name) **has** permission to participate in abstinence classes.

_____ Parent / Guardian Signature

_____ (girl's name) **does not have** permission to participate in abstinence classes.

_____ Parent/ Guardian Signature

I will provide transportation for _____ to and from the meeting. She will be picked up promptly at _____ (time) _____ (day & date) meeting. I understand that _____ [your group's name] does not provide transportation to or from meetings.

_____ Parent / Guardian Signature_____ Date

PERSONAL INFORMATION & INTEREST FORM

Name _____

Parent's Name _____

Address _____ Apt. # ____

City _____ State _____ Zip _____

Phone _____ Cell _____

In case of emergency contact: Name _____ Phone _____

Age _____ Date of Birth _____

School attended _____

Grade _____

Please list activities you wish to participate in below:

Please list any difficulties you are having either personal or at school:

Have you dropped out of school?   Yes   or   No
If yes, would you like for someone to help you re-enroll.

What would you like to do in this group?

Have you accepted Jesus as Lord and Savior of your life? Yes or No

Have you been baptized?   Yes   or   No

Would you like to learn more about God?   Yes   or   No

GEMMS PLEDGE

We are GEMMS,

Gifted, Elegant, Motivated, Magnificent Sisters –

We will honor, love and respect God and ourselves.

We will always be considerate of others

We strive for excellence in everything we do.

We are beautiful, intelligent, unique,

special creations of God.

–Michelle Easley

◆
CHAPTER 2
I Love Me – A Self Esteem Workshop

PRECIOUS JEWEL

> *"For we are God's workmanship, created in Christ Jesus to do good works, which God prepared in advance for us to do."*
> *Ephesians 2:10*

> *"Always be a first rate version of yourself instead of a second rate version of somebody else."*
> *–Judy Garland*

GATEWAY

Most girls feel the pressure to look like what they see on television, in movies and magazines. They never stop to think that most of the pictures have been digitally altered. Their expectations are unrealistic. The world places a great deal of emphasis on how one looks on the outside. Many images are over-sexualized. Girls are spinning in a whirlwind of confusion because they receive many mixed messages. You must be thin to be beautiful, have hair to your waist, and wear tight, revealing clothing. Many girls do not have positive self-images. They began to worry about their weight at early ages. Research states that one out of every one hundred young women between the ages of ten and twenty has anorexia and this is only one of the possible manifestations of low self-esteem.[1] You are charged with helping these girls develop positive, healthy self images. They must appreciate, value and love themselves from the inside out.

MIXER
GETTING TO KNOW MY SISTERS

It will be crucial that everyone get to know each other, adults and girls. In an effort to encourage conversation and sharing you will need to help everyone interact. This activity will be done at the very first session only or if you have an influx of new members.

For this activity you will prepare mini-cards in advance.

- Purchase two sets of inexpensive stickers, and a few sheets of brightly colored card stock paper.
- Cut the paper into two-inch squares and place one sticker on each card.
- Make sure each card has a sticker with an exact match.
- Mix the cards together and pass them out to the girls.
- Have the girls get up and find the person with the matching sticker.

Each girl will be responsible for introducing the girl with the matching sticker. You may want to tell them to share some specific information with the group before hand. For example, they should find out their partner's name, place of birth, birthday, school attending, grade, number of brothers and sisters, future goals and an interesting or funny fact about her. This usually gets things loosened up.

ECHOES
Sisters' Circle of Love

- Have the girls form a circle.
- You serve as the first volunteer.
- Go to the center of the circle.
- Have each girl in the circle say something positive about the person in the middle, in this case the person is you.
- They may say, "I like the way your hair looks," or "You have a beautiful smile."
- Each girl in the group will take turns moving to the inside of the circle.
- At the end, ask the girls if they noticed how the person on the inside of the circle smiled and how it felt to receive compliments. Let them know they should go out of their way each day to say something nice about someone else, if only one thing.

Footprints

- Have each girl take off her shoes. This really gets your group animated.
- Have one person trace the foot of another on a sheet of paper.
- Tell the girls to cut out their paper foot.
- Each girl will then write her name in the center of her foot and list five strengths on the front and five weaknesses or areas of needed improvement on the back.
- Decorate the paper foot using colored pencils, markers, glue, sequins, whatever you like.

Let the girls know their weaknesses will not be displayed but explain how even though our weaknesses exist in real life, they are often concealed from others. You want to make sure the girls understand that we are all far from perfect, having weaknesses is okay, and we work on our weaknesses over time. Each girl may then present her foot to the group, sharing weaknesses and strengths. Make a foot display for everyone to see. Of course, only volunteers will present and share, never force any girl to participate.

Birthday Club

At the first meeting initiate the Birthday Club as a monthly event. What better way is there to celebrate a person than to recognize her birthday? Designate one meeting per month to celebrate birthdays of persons born that month. This could be at the beginning or the end of the month. Bring cake, cupcakes, punch or cookies; whatever your budget allows. Sing "Happy Birthday" to the birthday girls and present them with inexpensive tokens such as poems or personalized birthday greetings. Have fun. It's a celebration.

My Best Me

- Have girls fold paper in threes (like a tri-fold brochure).

- Have each girl decorate the front flap with their name in any manner they want.

- Then have them open the brochure.

- Call out the following categories: my best feature, my proudest moment, favorite thing to do, something I'm good at, my role model is, my career goal...

- Have them list these categories on the inside. After the categories are listed the girls should write an answer. All answers must be positive. Give them a few minutes.

- Call time and tell them to fold up the brochure and paper clip it shut. Everyone should pass their brochure to the person on their right.

- When the next girl receives the brochure, she must note who it came from (they can look at the front flap), turn it over unopened, and write a positive comment about that person on the back.

- Repeat the process of passing it to the right and having them write a positive comment on the back until everyone has signed and the girls have their original brochure back.

- Each girl should silently read what was written about her.

- Have a discussion about what it was like to read things others have written.

- You may also discuss compliments: Why is it nice to be complimented? How does it make you feel to receive a compliment? Was it easy or hard to think of something positive to write about each other?

- Have volunteers share what was written on their brochures.

- Encourage girls to keep the brochure and take it home to reread when they may be feeling down about themselves or having a difficult day.

Rumor Game

The purpose of this activity is to illustrate how rumors and whispers can mislead others. Negative talk can lead to a decrease in self-esteem if the individual allows it to happen.

- Have everyone in the room make a circle. The leader whispers a phrase to the person next to her. That person whispers to the next person and so on until the last person in the circle has heard what was said.

- The leader has a written sentence in hand and holds it up for all to see as the last person announces what is said.
- Possible phrases to pass along: God loves each and every one of us; Jesus is the only way and the only answer; Love your neighbor; help those in need even if you only have a little to give.

Handprints
Make individual handprints:

- Select paper

- Trace your hand

- Write the following on each finger:
   1. An accomplishment you are proud of
   2. Something you admire about yourself
   3. Something you can do to help someone else
   4. What makes you unique
   5. Your favorite hobby

- Now decorate your hand by adding designs, shapes, lines, etc.

- Allow volunteers to present their hands and explain them to the group. Put the handprints on display.

MILESTONES

People tend to internalize more deeply when they write things down. A message has greater staying power when it is written. Writing also helps one to process and work through personal issues. Encourage girls to be truthful, candid and introspective when journaling. You may use copies of the pages that appear at the end of this chapter. Create a non-threatening environment where they are free to express themselves in a truthful manner with the knowledge that they will not be judged by their peers or adult leaders.
Have each person sign and recite the *Pledge of Confidentiality,* which is located at the end of the chapter.

Discuss the significance of this session's Precious Jewel scripture, as it applies to the topic being explored. Emphasize the fact that all of God's children are unique and special in every way. Let them know that diversity is valued and appreciated. Present the following example for thought: How many people love eating chocolate ice cream? How much fun do you think it would be to eat only chocolate ice cream for the rest of your life? I don't think we would enjoy that. That's why it is important that you value your uniqueness. Each of you has something special to share with the world. Encourage a verbal exchange and questions. Get the girls to express their concerns.

MAGNET

If you can get your parents to come in, conduct a quick ten-minute session with them. Have girls share the Bible verse and their decorated footprints with the parents. Ask the parents to share what it was like when they were teens, specifically how they viewed themselves. If actually getting parents in proves to be too difficult, provide each parent with a *Pearls for Parents* handout and send it home with each girl.

Pearls for Parents

- Watch what you say about yourself and your daughter. Don't focus on negative attributes such as, "I weigh too much" or "You need to lose weight."

- Model expected behavior in speech and action.

- Expose your daughter to successful, positive role models.

- Respond to your daughter with love and patience. Let her know that failure is not the end of the world but an opportunity to get up and try again.

- Don't let stereotypes rule your household. Allow your daughter to fix the car or work in the yard.

- Encourage your daughter to excel in math and science. Never accept her saying that she "just can't do math" or "doesn't get science." Get her extra help in school if needed.

- Tell your daughter its okay to speak her mind (if done respectfully).

- Encourage your daughter to get involved in sports and other physical activity.

SANCTUARY

Present each girl with a flower, carnation or rose, (any flower is fine), and tell them to notice how beautiful each one is, yet no two are exactly alike. They are just as beautiful and unique as the flowers they hold.

Sister's Circle

Form a circle and hold hands for your closing prayer. Ask for prayer requests. Have a girl read the closing suggested prayer below or make up her own.

Dear God,
Thank you for our uniqueness. The way you have made us makes this world a better place. Help us to glorify your creation in all that we do and say. Strengthen us as we work to improve ourselves. Keep us ever mindful that we are special, precious GEMMS in your sight.
Amen

GEMMS CONFIDENTIALITY PLEDGE

I _____ (name) will honor, love and respect myself. I will be considerate of others and respect their right to privacy. I will show love for my sisters by not repeating anything that is shared in our meetings. I will not gossip or discuss any private or personal matters outside of our group (except with a caring, trusted adult, parent, caregiver or guardian).

_____   _____

Signature   Date

MILESTONES

<u>Precious Jewel</u>

"For we are God's workmanship, created in Christ Jesus to do good works, which God prepared in advance for us to do." Ephesians 2:10

Use this page to write about the significance of this Precious Jewel as it relates to your personal self-esteem. Remember to be reflective and honest as you journal.

CHAPTER 3
Looking Good, Feeling Great
Beauty With A Purpose

PRECIOUS JEWEL

"Charm is deceptive, and beauty is fleeting;
but a woman who fears the Lord is to be praised."
Proverbs 31:30

"You are most beautiful when God's love shines
through you and illuminates the world around you."
–Michelle Easley

GATEWAY

(Set up a display of magazine pictures that depicts a cross-section of beauty. Several ethnicities should be included.)

Are you really a size 2? Is that your real hair? Are your teeth super, pearly white? Are your eyes emerald green? Is how we look important? The answer is a resounding YES! Everyone wants to feel confident that the image she sees in the mirror is pleasing to others as well as herself. Our bodies are a wonderful gift entrusted to us by God. Our task is to maintain and preserve them through sensible diet, exercise and hygiene. The better we look, the better we feel. The better we feel, the better we act. A beautiful YOU begins on the inside and is reflected on the outside through your skin, hair, smile and disposition. Maybe some of us want to have the body of the Venus de Milo, a smile like Mona Lisa, hair like Cleopatra, a body like Beyonce, skin like Eva Langoria, Faith Hill and Gabrielle Union but our beauty regimen has a higher purpose: to honor God with our bodies and minds.

MIXER
What is beauty?
Allow ten minutes for each girl to write her definition of BEAUTY on an index card. Collect the cards and

anonymously share some of the definitions. Look at the magazine photos as you share. Are the pictures in sync with what the girls are saying? How does the scripture provide guidance for defining beauty? What virtue does it encourage? (humility)

ECHOES

How Healthy Is My Lifestyle?
Each girl should do a self-assessment using the questionnaire, "How Healthy Is My Lifestyle?" Scores can be calculated quickly to reveal a snapshot of health habits. See the end of the chapter for the questionnaire.

Beauty & Wellness Seminar
Present an in-depth seminar on building self-esteem through personal hygiene and well-being. Important information and practical tips on diet, exercise, body and skin care will be shared. Presentation design can be found at the end of the chapter.

MILESTONES

In the first activity of this session the girls wrote their definition of beauty. Ask them to consider everything that has been said about healthy lifestyles. Share the following questions for reflection: Has your definition changed? How? Why? Do you have a responsibility to God to be as beautiful as you can be? Consider the scripture Proverbs 31:30 and I Corinthians 6:19 – 20 and write a letter to God about your feelings concerning his greatest creation----YOU.

MAGNET

Invite mothers to allow their daughters to give them a facial or manicure (under the guidance of adult supervision). Provide small gifts of beauty and hygiene products as tokens of appreciation, such as pocket tissue, hand lotion, hand sanitizer, lip gloss, body powder, etc. These items may be purchased inexpensively at discount retail outlets.

Pearls for Parents

• Your daughters model and mimic what they see. Be good to yourself by taking care of what God has blessed you with.

• Have a healthy breakfast.

• Hum a tune as you brush your teeth. Relax.

• Always buckle up in the car.

• De-stress by listening to soothing music on your way home.

• Stay hydrated, drink plenty of water.

• Protect your skin from sun and environmental damage.

• Exercise.

• Eat a nutritional dinner.

• Use a facial cleanser and moisturizer every night.

• Brush and floss.

• Get a good night's sleep.

SANCTUARY

Form a prayer circle to close the session.

Heavenly Father,
Thank you for giving us the precious gift of wholesome, healthy bodies. Give us the wisdom to preserve and protect these holy temples. Let everything we say and do honor you always.
Amen

Additional Precious Jewel

"Do you not know that your body is a temple of the Holy Spirit, who is in you, whom you have received from God? You are not your own; you were bought at a price. Therefore honor God with your body."

I Corinthians 6: 19 - 20

Beauty and Wellness Seminar Presentation Design

Discussion Guide

*Encourage honest, introspective thinking and interaction as you discuss the following topics with your group.

DIET
What is junk food?
Burgers, fries, chips, candy, cookies, and sodas qualify as non-nutritious edibles. Limit snacks and fast foods to control weight, increase energy and maintain healthy skin.

What is healthy food?
Fruits, vegetables, chicken, fish, lean meats, whole grains, milk, water are the flip side of junk. They are essential for a wholesome lifestyle.

EXERCISE
How often should you exercise?
To maintain a fit and healthy body exercise is a MUST. At least three times a week is a great start. Do you need a trainer or a gym to get in shape? Absolutely not. Exercise is as simple as walking, biking, skating, running, jumping rope, dancing or playing ball. Just get moving and do it consistently. Don't forget the importance of good posture whether you are sitting or standing. Perfect stature can make you feel like the regal queen you are.

BODY
How often should you bathe or shower?
Bathing or showering at least once a day is essential, more may be necessary depending on your activities. Use a mild soap or body wash and always follow up with deodorant and body lotion.

HAIR
How often should you shampoo your hair?
Hair should be shampooed as often as needed. After shampooing use a conditioner to keep hair manageable and soft. Choose a style that is flattering to you and easy to care for on a daily basis.

NAILS
What nail care is best for you?
Clean, neat natural nails are always a winner. They are more economical to maintain. Use a nail brush to clean, shape with a file and apply an attractive shade of nail enamel. Acrylic nails may be an option for older girls. Keep in mind that they have been known to cause problems in some people. If products and

utensils are not properly sanitized a fungus may result. Face it, girls, natural is nicer (and cheaper) any day.

TEETH

How often should you brush?

Good dental hygiene is essential to good health and self-esteem. Brush at least twice a day (morning/night) and always after a meal if possible and don't forget to floss. Regular dental visits will guarantee that perfect smile forever.

COMPLEXION

Can a person look at your face and tell what is going on in your life? Well, they may not be able to get a whole picture, but they can get a snapshot. They will be able to tell if you eat a healthy diet or junk food, if you smoke, drink alcohol or do drugs and if you get enough sleep. HOW? If you abuse your body it will show first in your face----pimples, sores, dark spots, wrinkles and bags under your eyes. How do you prevent this and always look and feel your best? (If you have more serious skin problems, such as severe acne, you may need to consult a dermatologist.) It's simple:

- Eat nutritious food

- Drink plenty of water

- Get adequate rest

- Exercise regularly

- Cleanse your face properly

A **skin care demonstration** should follow this presentation and discussion. See the next page for a sample demonstration.

SKIN CARE DEMONSTRATION

A beautiful you begins with clean, clear skin. Keeping it radiant and glowing is as easy as 1 2 3, it only takes a few minutes. This hands-on demonstration will teach you the basics that will last a lifetime.

You will need:
Wash cloths and warm water
Mild facial cleaner
Gentle moisturizer

Procedure:
Apply cleanser/wash face thoroughly
Rinse carefully
Pat dry
Apply moisturizer
Repeat this process morning and night

If parents or other adults are present a demonstration of proper make-up application can complete the seminar. This demo would include correct use of foundation, blush, mascara, eye shadow and lipstick. Older girls may want to participate. This session is an excellent opportunity to involve outside mentors and consultants from major products companies like Avon, Mary Kay and Jafra.

Cheap and Handy Alternatives
Can you brush your teeth if you just ran out of tooth paste? Sure. Just look in the kitchen cabinet and get some baking soda and a pinch of salt. With a wet tooth brush you can have a clean, sparkling smile in seconds. Throughout the ages these simple alternatives have saved the day many times.

NO...	USE ...
Deodorant	Baking soda paste
Breath Freshener	Whole cloves (2 or 3 in mouth for a minute, do not swallow)
Moisturizer	Baby oil
Lotion	Cooking oil
Lip gloss	Vaseline (add a few drops of vanilla flavoring)
Full body massage	Bath Brush (scrub body from top to bottom to invigorate your skin)

Finally, your body is a temple; love it, respect it, cherish it and thank GOD for it.

How healthy is my lifestyle?

Answer YES or NO

1. _____ Physically and emotionally do you feel healthy?

2. _____ Are you rested when you wake up in the morning?

3. _____ Do you eat plenty of fruits, vegetables, whole grains and lean meats?

4. _____ Do you drink at least eight glasses of water a day?

5. _____ Is regular exercise a part of your weekly routine?

6. _____ Is your weight appropriate for your bone structure?

7. _____ Do you visit the doctor regularly?

8. _____ Is your dental hygiene keeping your smile beautiful?

9. _____ Do you avoid smoking, alcohol and illegal drugs?

10. _____ Do you take time to get in touch with yourself each day?

If you answered YES to at least 7 questions you are on the right path to a healthy lifestyle.

MILESTONES

Precious Jewel

"Do you not know that your body is a temple of the Holy Spirit, who is in you, whom you have received from God? You are not your own; you were bought at a price. Therefore honor God with your body." I Corinthians 6: 19 - 20

"Charm is deceptive, and beauty is fleeting; but a woman who fears the Lord is to be praised." Proverbs 31:30

Consider the Precious Jewel printed above and Proverbs 31:30. Write a letter to God about your feelings concerning his greatest creation, you. Has your definition of beauty changed? What is your definition of beauty? Do you have a responsibility to God to be beautiful on the inside as well as the outside?

CHAPTER 4
Getting Where I Want To Be
Life Mapping/Goal Setting/Career Choices

PRECIOUS JEWEL

"Commit to the Lord whatever you do, and your plans will succeed."
Proverbs 16:3

"The big secret in life is that there is no big secret. Whatever
your goal you can get there if you're willing to work."
–Oprah Winfrey

"The tragedy of life doesn't lie in not reaching your goal.
The tragedy lies in having no goal to reach."
–Benjamin E. Mays

GATEWAY

No one has a crystal ball that tells the future, but God knew his plan for the life of each young woman before she was born. He placed desires and interests in their hearts. He gave them special gifts and abilities. Each young woman is unique. Have you ever wondered if the next Oprah Winfrey, Maya Angelou, Halle Berry, Condeleeza Rice, Hillary Clinton, Shirley Franklin, Diane Sawyer, Mae Jemison, Judge Glenda Hatchett, Gloria Estefan, Jennifer Lopez, Kimora Lee Simmons, Celine Dion or Dr. Julie Gerberding could be in your midst? These women began as girls and undoubtedly as girls with big dreams. Each girl has a dream, even if she can't articulate it. This is where you come in. You will assist the girls in capturing their dreams and breaking them down into realistic goals. Of course, it's not as simple as that. It takes hard work, dedication, faith and prayers, but these dreams can become a reality.

It all begins with success in school. A good education is the foundation for life. Through learning one can achieve not just material wealth or worldly goods but success as a true child of God. Each girl will need to build her own house. Her foundation will be a strong spiritual life, a rock solid relationship with God, a fervent prayer life, and a true understanding and knowledge of the Bible. To this she will add a pursuit of academic excellence. She will strive to succeed in school. From here the sky is the limit. She can choose to run her own company, start her own school, work in an established organization, or do mission work. The purpose of this chapter is to guide young women as they live, encouraging them to actively map out their life goals and plan for a successful future.

MIXER
What's My Job? What's it worth?
The objective of the game is to explore the wide range of available careers and open the dialogue about non-traditional careers for women.

- Locate the career cards at the end of the chapter. Each card has a different occupation printed on it. There are a wide range of careers, some requiring a college education or beyond and some requiring vocational or other training. Careers do not reflect any gender bias. Girls should be encouraged to pursue whatever they are interested in.

- Have half of the girls select a career card and stand in a line at the front of the room.

- The other half of the girls will get a salary card.

- The girls will need to match their salary card to the correct career card.

- After all girls have paired up, call out the correct salary for each career. A chart detailing each career and its matching salary can be found at the end of the chapter.

- Direct the girls' attention to the fact that some "traditional" jobs for women such as cashier, waitress, and child care worker pay minimum wage, while "nontraditional" jobs such as aircraft mechanic, plumber, electrician and aircraft pilot pay substantially more.

- Encourage the girls to discuss the following: Do I use my hands in my work? Could I do this if I only have a high school diploma? Does this job pay a living wage? Will I need to complete college or graduate work to attain this job? What type of career most interests me? You must first see it if you are ever to be it. The girls must be able to visualize themselves as successful, in school, at home, now or ten years in the future.

ECHOES
Road Map to Success
Each girl should complete the *Road Map to Success*. If the girls desire, they can present their Road Maps to the group. The *Road Map to Success* can be found at the end of the chapter. This document forces the girls to think about what their future goals are and the steps they need to take to ensure these goals become a reality.

Steps of Life
Each girl should complete the *Steps of Life*. In this activity she will be able to set goals for her life. She can also think about what she needs to do to actually attain these goals. *Steps of Life* can be found at the end of the chapter. This exercise provides the girls an additional opportunity to plan for an awesome future.

Choices
Let's face it, many young people look for what they think is the easy way out. They opt to make quick money without hard work. It is critical that you create a safe, non-threatening, non-judgmental environment

in which to have this discussion. Some girls may feel that a life being an adult dancer, adult escort, lingerie model, prostitute or drug dealer would provide tremendous financial comfort; however, they don't understand the serious downside of these lifestyles. Complete *Choices*, located at the end of the chapter and really delve into the negative aspects of each choice. Many young women have made these choices and suffered from physical violence, drug addiction, shame, disgrace, disease and death.

Invite a young lady to your group to give a personal testimony about her life. Perhaps this young woman was incarcerated, or a former adult dancer, she can tell a powerful story. Let the girls know that even if they do slip and find themselves in a less than pleasing place, God will forgive them and restore them. They can repent for their sins. Real repentance is shown when actions and behaviors are changed.

Celebration of Success

This is your opportunity to plan a party, and who doesn't love a party? Girls will meet successful females from a broad range of occupations - entrepreneurs, professional women, educators, college and graduate students. They will participate in an informational/question and answer session.

Here's what you need to do:
- Decide on a date and have the girls write letters or create invitations for guest speakers. You should send out your invitations at least a month in advance. Allow enough time to receive responses. You may target members of your church, community members or personal acquaintances. You may consider contacting the local radio and television stations. Invite on-air personalities to serve as speakers. Other ideas for guests include authors, local elected officials, business owners, teachers at nearby colleges, universities, high schools, elementary schools, principals, doctors, dentists, hair stylists, nail technicians, doctors, lawyers, postal workers, engineers, scientists, musicians, etc.

- It is a good idea to inform your guests that they will be part of a panel and that they should be prepared to discuss their careers, ie, education and preparation required, duties involved, salary and other interesting information.

- Set time limits for each speaker in advance and communicate these limits to your guests. Allow at least thirty minutes at the end of your session for questions and answers.

- Allot at least ninety minutes for the entire celebration so that each person will have an opportunity to speak. Make sure that girls write their questions down and ask them after each guest has presented. You may need to adjust your time depending on the number of confirmed guests you have. Ask your guests to come with a small token for each girl, perhaps a pen with their company's name printed on it.

- Prepare your meeting space in advance. Provide bottled water for your guests and certificates of appreciation. Depending on your budget, it's always a nice touch to provide light refreshments, such as fresh fruit. Decorate with balloons, have the girls make posters or create banners that read, "Celebration of Success".

- End by having one of your girls thank each guest and present her with a certificate of appreciation.

• As a follow-up activity have each girl write a thank you letter to all participants.

MILESTONES

Discuss the significance of the verse, Proverbs 16:3. The girls must know they are not just sending up prayer requests and waiting for their fulfillment. They must actively work to make their future goals a reality. It is imperative that they plan and prepare a *Road Map to Success*. God will meet them as they complete the journey.

Additionally, they should write about their chosen career: what was chosen, why it was chosen and what they have to do to achieve this career goal. Finally, they should tell what personal satisfaction they may receive from this choice and how this choice will glorify God.

MAGNET

Have parents come in and be active listeners as the girls share their future goals. Parents may want to share what their careers are or their future goals. Parents must sign a *Pledge of Support* to help their daughters in every way possible. The pledge can be found at the end of the chapter.

Pearls for Parents

- Talk to your daughter about setting positive, substantial goals for her life.

- Support her as she works to attain these goals.

- Provide her with positive learning experiences, i.e. enroll her in dance if she states she wants to be a dancer, send her to science summer camp if she wants to become a doctor.

- Regularly discuss choices and consequences, for example, if you don't study you will fail the test which may lead to you failing the class which could ultimately delay your graduation from high school.

- Tell her about mistakes you made and what you learned from them.

- Let your life be a positive example of setting goals and reaching them.

SANCTUARY

Present each girl with her framed *Road Map to Success*. Tell the girls to look at their Road Maps on a regular basis but particularly when life gets difficult.

Prayer Circle
Close with a prayer, accept prayer requests.

Dear God,
Help us to find our way, recognize your plan for our lives and to do your will. Please take away all selfishness and confusion which may cloud our view of you. Make our lives a living testimony of your goodness and grace. Grant that we may glorify your name in all that we do.
Amen

Additional Precious Jewel
  "All hard work brings a profit, but mere talk leads only to poverty." Proverbs 14:23

JOB CARDS
Cut along lines

CASHIER	**DENTIST**
WAITRESS	**DENTAL HYGIENIST**
CHILD CARE WORKER	**AIRCRAFT MECHANIC**
PLUMBER	**TEACHER**
REGISTERED NURSE	**AUTO MECHANIC**

ELECTRICIAN	PHARMACIST
OBSTETRICIAN	ANESTHESIOLOGIST
CONSTRUCTION MANAGER	PHYSICAL THERAPIST
PHYSICIAN ASSISTANT	PHARMACY AIDE
DENTAL ASSISTANT	BUS DRIVER

PARAMEDIC	GYNECOLOGIST
AEROSPACE ENGINEER	PHYSICIST
CHEMICAL ENGINEER	ATTORNEY
MECHANICAL ENGINEER	PARALEGAL
COMPUTER SOFTWARE ENGINEER	COSMETOLOGIST

COMPUTER SYSTEMS ANALYST	ADMINISTRATIVE ASSISTANT
AIR TRAFFIC CONTROLLER	AIRCRAFT PILOT

SALARY CARDS
Cut along lines

$27,710	**$35,568**
$50,993	**$53,813**
$50,236	**$79,740**
$66,460	**$87,450**
$94,900	**$39,130**

$30,930	$34,970
$38,030	$102,030
$129,250	$10,712
$14,040	$15,267
$45,282	$41,288

$41,400	**$39,130**
$52,330	**$32,448**
$42,282	**$58,344**
$129,250	**$203,270**
$14,040	**$84,900**

$45,282	$69,870
$41,400	$69,410
$52,330	$60,180
$28,340	$18,249

WHAT'S MY JOB? WHAT'S IT WORTH?

Salary Guide

Paramedic	$ 27,710
Aerospace Engineer	50,993
Chemical Engineer	53,813
Mechanical Engineer	50,236
Computer Software Engineer	79,740
Computer Systems Analyst	66,460
Physicist	87,450
Attorney	94,900
Paralegal	39,130
Cosmetologist	30,390
Administrative Assistant	34,970
Graphic Designer	38,030
Air traffic controller	102,030
Aircraft Pilot	129,250
Bus Driver (City)	35,568
Cashier	10,712
Waitress	14,040
Child Care Worker	15,267
Aircraft Mechanic	45,282
Plumber	41,288
Teacher	41,400
Registered Nurse	52,330
Auto Mechanic	32,448
Electrician	42,286
Dental Hygienist	58,344
Dentist	129,920
Gynecologist/Obstetrician	203,270
Pharmacist	84,900
Construction Manager	69,870
Anesthesiologist	259,948
Physician Assistant	69,140
Physical Therapist	60,180
Dental Assistant	28,330
Pharmacy Aide	18,429

Salaries stated are starting salaries and information was retrieved from Occupational Outlook Handbook 2004, U.S. Department of Labor Bureau of Labor Statistics, http://www.bls.gov

ROAD MAP TO SUCCESS

This school year I will make grades of _____ in every subject. In order to achieve this I will do these three things:

MY FUTURE GOAL IS TO

_____

I WOULD LIKE TO ATTEND _____ COLLEGE/
UNIVERSITY/TECHNICAL OR VOCATIONAL SCHOOL.

IN ORDER TO REACH THIS GOAL I PLAN TO DO THE FOLLOWING THINGS:

_____

_____

If things in my life start to go wrong or if I feel overwhelmed I will …

_____

_____

I PROMISE TO BE DRUG, ALCOHOL & TOBACCO FREE!!

_____   _____

Signature   Date

SUCCESS
ONE WAY

THE STEPS OF LIFE

Complete the steps of life. Write the goals you wish to reach in 5 years, 10 years and your plans for making them happen!

In ten years I will…

In five years I will…

These are the things I must do to make it all happen…

I can do all things through Christ who strengthens me. Philippians 4:13 (NASB)

CHOICES

DEATH

MONEY

STRIPPER

JAIL

HAPPINESS

DRUG DEALER

HIV/AIDS

SHAME

SELFWORTH

VIOLENCE

PEACE OF MIND

THIEF

LOSS OF FREEDOM

DRUG ADDICTION

DEPRESSION

ALCOHOLISM

CONTENTMENT

WEALTH

SECURITY

LOVE

STABILITY

ANXIETY

HONOR

EMBARRASSMENT

SEXUALLY TRANSMITTED DISEASES

Circle the words that come to mind when you consider being a nurse. **Underline** the words that come to mind when you think of being an adult dancer, in other words a stripper. Look carefully at the uncircled words. Do they reflect a life you want to have?

"Dishonest money dwindles away, but he who gathers money little by little makes it grow."
Proverbs 13:11, NIV

GEMMS PARENT'S PLEDGE OF SUPPORT

I _____ (parent's name) pledge to support my daughter in all endeavors. I will provide her with opportunities to grow and develop. I will love her unconditionally yet provide her with limits and boundaries. I will empower her to make intelligent, wise decisions. I will help her establish a solid spiritual foundation upon which she can build.

_____   _____

Parent's Signature   Date

MILESTONES

Precious Jewel

"Commit to the Lord whatever you do, and your plans will succeed." Proverbs 16:3

Consider the Precious Jewel printed above and write about what it means to you. Also write about your future career goals, why you selected this career, what you need to do to achieve this goal and how your choice will glorify God

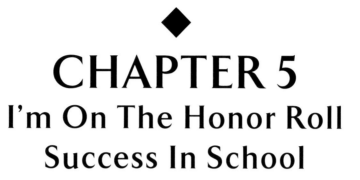

CHAPTER 5
I'm On The Honor Roll
Success In School

PRECIOUS JEWEL

"I can do all things through Him who strengthens me."
(Philippians 4: 13 New American Standard Bible)

"When you educate a man you educate an individual,
but when you educate a woman, you educate a nation".
–Johnetta Cole

GATEWAY

According to the Center for Educational Statistics in 2005, 488,000 students dropped out of high school. Put another way, 1 in 3 students in the class of 2006 will not graduate. According to a study sponsored by the Bill and Melinda Gates Foundation public schools graduate 69.6% of their students. This means that 30% of the students are not graduating.[2] Minority students are in an even more perilous position. The drop out rate in 2005 for African Americans was 10.4% and 22.4% for Hispanic Americans.[3] What does this really mean for the young ladies that sit in front of you? Some may actually be drop outs and others might be thinking about dropping out. Don't just assume because you work with girls in more affluent neighborhoods or with successful, educated parents that they are immune to this problem. Unfortunately, this just isn't the case. When a young lady drops out she is more likely to end up on some form of public assistance in her lifetime. She is 3 times more likely to be unemployed or underemployed than a college graduate. She's more likely to have a job earning minimum wage. She'll earn almost ten thousand dollars less than a high school graduate.[4] She'll look forward to a possible life of poverty, receive poorer health services, and unfortunately face an increased likelihood of incarceration.

Why should this be significant to you? It means you are the critical link. You are the person to change the course of her life. Your goal is to help this young lady rethink her decision about dropping out. Making sure that other girls never even begin to consider dropping out is your mission. The difference between success and possible failure is in your hands. You have the power to change tomorrows.

You are charged with the task of getting these young ladies to think logically, critically and deeply about the future they face. You must empower them to develop conscious, deliberate thoughts about their lives. They must begin to take responsibility for their own futures. School success is not just a chapter in this book; it's not just a cliché for the moment. It is essentially one of the most critical components of preparation for the future. Failure in school can translate into a series of struggles. Of course, education does not guarantee a life of happiness, peace and wealth but in today's competitive, global marketplace a high school diploma is essential. GEMMS must understand that education is the key to a brighter future. They must be encouraged not only to complete high school but to go on and pursue a college degree and advanced degrees. School success is not optional, it is required!

MIXER
Let's Go Shopping

Divide the girls into four groups. Give group one – $5, group two – $10, group three – $15 and group four – $20. If possible use real money. At the beginning of the session you will need to make sure that the girls know that the money is just for the game and it should not leave the room; it is not theirs to keep. If it is not possible to use real money just use money from a board game.

- Place items on a table. Items can include toothpaste, soap, deodorant, a hair brush, boxes of cereal, juice boxes, macaroni, milk, bread, a pair of Nike or other name brand tennis shoes, cell phone with a average monthly cost attached and other items that you feel represent things you need and want in daily life.

- Clearly label each item with a realistic price.

- Tell them that they are going to shop for the basic necessities of life.

- Have each group buy the items and return to their area.

- Have each group stand up and tell what items they were able to buy and why they chose those items.

- After each group has presented lead the girls in a discussion. Guiding questions could be:

  1. What was different about the number of items that group one could buy compared to group four?

  2. How would life be different if you earned $ 6.00/hr vs. $18.00/hr. vs. $100,000 per year?

  3. Imagine that you have a child. How does this affect the amount of money you need to live each month?

It should become clear as you dialogue with the girls that the more money you have the more you are able to buy. This means later in life you would be able to pay for a place to live, have a car to drive, food to eat and perhaps pay for an occasional movie and dinner out. We want the girls to realize that earnings dictate lifestyle and that education dictates earnings. We are by no means promoting material wealth as the end all we simply want the girls to be able to sustain themselves in the future without reliance on public assistance.

ECHOES

Budget Practice

Each girl will complete the monthly budget sheet which can be found at the end of the chapter. Discuss minimum wages. Now discuss wages for such careers as massage therapists, doctors, lawyers, engineers, teachers, physician assistants, chefs, nail technicians, hair stylists, and entrepreneurs. Make it plain for the girls; you must succeed in school to succeed in life. Education is the foundation for everything! Once you have it no one can take it away. Help the girls to see just how much it costs to live from month to month, to cover the basic expenses. This exercise also shows the girls just how important math is.

Grade Gala

This activity can only be done if you have developed a great deal of trust between the adult facilitators and the girls. This is an excellent way to get the parents involved. Invite the parents to this meeting, if they are unable to come have them sign a written parental permission slip giving you permission to see the girls' grades. Have each girl show you her mid-semester and end of semester report cards. Some girls may be uncomfortable with this, don't force them. Tell them that you all will work together as partners to achieve school success.

Praise the girls that have made As and Bs. You may even want to give them a certificate (located at the end of the chapter) to celebrate their successes. If they are on the honor roll give them a special recognition, perhaps a rose or a book of inspirational quotes. Help your girls create a plan to improve any grades that are C or lower. You may want to ask such questions as: Are you turning in all of your homework, classroom assignments and projects on time? Are you completing lab work if that is required? Are you participating in class? Are you positive and respectful towards the teacher? Are you having any behavioral issues? Are you talking too much in class? Not paying attention? Do you pass tests in the class? Have you told the teacher that you are having trouble? Can you ask him/her to give you extra credit assignments? Is tutoring available? Have the girls to create an individualized 5-step plan to improve their grade in each subject. It may be as simple as studying more for tests or it may involve seeking a tutor. A sample five-step plan and *School Success Tip Sheet* can be found at the end of the chapter.

Tutoring Program

You may need to create and maintain a tutoring program. Each adult facilitator may serve one to five girls. If you feel you have the expertise you may also tutor girls in various subject areas. If not, you may seek community or church members to serve as volunteers. Invite college and high school students, retired educators and others to serves as tutors. **Note of Caution:** any time outsiders work with the girls you must exercise extreme caution. You are advised to do background checks and have a monitoring system in place. Make sure you provide orientation for the volunteers and set clear and concise guidelines and expectations. Do not allow the girls to give the volunteers too much personal information. Safety is a priority. Unfortunately, we live in a litigious society; as a result you must be ever mindful of the girl's safety and your own.

MILESTONES

Reflect on the Precious Jewel, Philippians 4:13. Tell how this scripture can help you as you work to meet all of your future goals.

MAGNET

Invite parents to the Grade Gala. Have them commit to supporting their daughters in their school endeavors. They can sign a pledge of support and recite the pledge aloud. A sample pledge can be found at the end of the chapter. Give each girl and her parent the *ABCs of School Success*.

Pearls for Parents

- Help your daughter become a critical thinker. This means she shouldn't just accept everything as presented. Encourage her to think deeply and always ask questions.

- Help your daughter to be organized. Make sure she has a quiet, well-lit place to study. Even if she doesn't have her own desk, the kitchen table will work. Turn off the television and radio.

- Ensure that your daughter has school supplies, not just at the beginning of the school year but throughout the year. Supplies include, but are not limited to, paper, pencils, pens, notebooks, folders, rulers, calculator, protractor, dictionary, thesaurus, atlas, scissors, and glue.

- Get your daughter a public library card and take her to the library on a regular basis. Journey through the sections of the library together. Read fiction, nonfiction, biographies, and how-to-books. Just read everything!

- Help with homework. If the subject matter is too hard for you, seek out a tutor. Perhaps a friend in the neighborhood or a church member may be willing to help for free.

- Visit your child's school often, not just when there is a problem. Get to know her teachers, the counselor and the principal. Let everyone know that you are an active part of your child's academic life.

- Show genuine interest in your daughter's study. For example, ask her to teach you a phrase in the foreign language she is studying.

- Encourage your daughter to study everyday. She should study more than the night before a major exam. Help her prioritize her activities. Limit time on the phone, watching TV and hanging out. Make studying the number one priority during the regular school year.

• Volunteer at your child's school. Even if you work all day try to donate a least a few minutes to work in your child's school or classroom. If possible take the day off and go on the field trip with her. Donate needed items to a teacher.

• Become an active member of the Parent Teacher Student Association at your daughter's school.

• Praise your daughter for all of her good work. Keep a scrapbook of memorable events, snapshots, awards and certificates.

• Create a loving home environment filled with patience. Let your daughter know that she is loved and valued even when she fails.

• Be your child's positive role model.

• Help your daughter create a balanced life. In addition to studying, she should participate in extracurricular activities at school and in the community. Ideas include, singing in the choir, taking dance, playing a sport or volunteering.

• Help your child develop a healthy and strong spiritual life. Take her to a place of worship on a consistent basis and encourage her to pray daily as you pray for her.

SANCTUARY

Form a prayer circle.

Father,
Thank you for granting us the opportunity to learn, explore and discover the wonders of the universe.
Education is a precious privilege that we are grateful to have. Guide us as we seek knowledge. Help us
to be successful both in school and out.
Amen

WHERE DID ALL MY MONEY GO?

Complete the monthly budget. Do a little research and find the **actual** cost of these items in the area where you live.

INCOME How much do I make each month?	AMOUNT
EXPENSES	
RENT	
Utilities	
Electricity	
Water	
Gas	
Telephone	
LIVING EXPENSES	
Groceries	
Eating Out	
Visits to the hair/nail salon	
Pocket Money	
Entertainment	
Clothing	
TITHE TO CHURCH (10%)	
DONATIONS TO CHARITY	
TRANSPORTATION	
Public transportation costs	
Car Payment	
Gas	
Maintenance/ Repairs	
Insurance	
DEBT	
Credit Cards	
OTHER EXPENSES	
Cable TV	
Magazine Subscriptions	
SAVINGS	
Investments	
Emergency funds	
OTHER	
DEFICIT/SURPLUS	

CERTIFICATE
OF
EXCELLENCE

_____

IS AWARDED THIS

CERTIFICATE

FOR ACADEMIC EXCELLENCE

THIS _____ DAY OF _____, _____

_____   _____

Signature   Date

IF YOU NEED TO IMPROVE YOUR GRADE:

5 STEP PLAN FOR SCHOOL SUCCESS

1. CONFERENCE WITH YOUR TEACHER

2. DEVOTE MORE TIME TO STUDYING

3. FIND A TUTOR

4. TRY GROUP STUDY WITH PEERS

5. HAVE YOUR TEACHER EVALUATE YOUR PERFORMANCE IN CLASS AT LEAST WEEKLY.

TOP 10 TIPS FOR SCHOOL SUCCESS

1. Be organized. Have a folder for every subject.

2. Be prepared. Have your paper, pens, and pencils, everyday that you go to school not just at the beginning of the year. Make sure your homework is done on time and all assignments are turned in.

3. Go to class with your books and ready to learn each day.

4. Study every night. Don't wait until the night before a major exam to cram.

5. Participate in class. Let the teacher know you are interested in learning.

6. Go above and beyond the minimum requirements.

7. Ask for help if you need it. If you don't understand something ask the teacher to explain it again. Go back after or before school if that's what it takes.

8. Read something everyday, a book, magazine or newspaper article. This builds your vocabulary and will ultimately increase your standardized test scores.

9. Set high goals for yourself. Strive to make an "A" in every class.

10. Get involved. Participate in extracurricular activities – be a cheerleader, play basketball, get in the drama club, play in the band or orchestra, sing in the chorus. Do something!

ABCs OF SCHOOL SUCCESS

Always aim high

Believe you can achieve

Concentrate on the task

Don't give up

Express yourself clearly

Face each challenge with confidence

Go the extra mile

Help someone along the way

Ignore distractions

Join a club

Know thyself

Listen to your elders

Memorize important facts

Never procrastinate

Open your mind to new ideas

Prepare to learn something new each day

Quell apathy

Read, read, read, read, read

Stay focused

Take good notes

Use your imagination

Value knowledge

Write it down

X-aggerate the positive

Yearn to learn

Zero in on your goal and make it happen!

MILESTONES

Precious Jewel

"I can do all things through Him who strengthens me."
(Philippians 4: 13 New American Standard Bible)

Reflect on the Precious Jewel printed above; write about how this scripture can help you as you work to meet your future goals. What are a few things you need to do now to reach your goals?

◆
CHAPTER 6
Service With A Smile: Serve Others

PRECIOUS JEWEL

"In everything I did, I showed you that by this kind of hard work we must help the weak, remembering the words the Lord Jesus himself said, 'It is more blessed to give than to receive.'"

Acts 20:35

"I have found that among its other benefits giving liberates the soul of the giver."

– Maya Angelou

GATEWAY

President John F. Kennedy spoke these words during his inaugural speech; "My fellow Americans, ask not what your country can do for you; ask what you can do for your country." Acts 20:35 tells us that "it is more blessed to give than to receive." In today's self-centered world many young people focus only on themselves - me, me, me, gimme, gimme, gimme. The world seems to uphold this type of behavior and glamorize the selfish approach through the music we listen to, movies we watch and commercials we take in.

Sometimes young people are burdened down with problems - problems at home, problems at school, and problems with friends. Shifting the focus from self to others can make a huge difference. Helping others can be an outlet or a temporary escape. It usually helps the giver as much or more than the receiver. Take for example, Oprah Winfrey's decision to build The Oprah Winfrey Leadership Academy in South Africa. Although she donated millions and created a spectacular institution of learning for girls she is quoted as saying on many different occasions that she received more from the girls than she ever could have given them. Something extraordinary happens when you decide to give and make a difference in someone else's life. As a leader, your journey will give you more than you ever thought possible.

As you read this some of you are probably thinking, "The girls I work with need all the help they can get. They are in no position to help anyone else." Perhaps you are working with economically disadvantaged girls or girls that have dropped out of school, are incarcerated or living in rural areas. Guess what? They can still help. All of us, regardless of our present circumstances, have God-given gifts, talents and abilities. You don't necessarily have to have money to make a positive difference. We're talking about getting your group, no matter how large or how small, involved in community service.

Community service is simply designing a project to meet a need in the community you serve. Community service projects promote civic responsibility and help to increase the self-esteem of all participants - the givers and the receivers.

Begin by asking your girls to write their own vision. What would they envision themselves doing to make a difference? Hopefully, they will come up with a workable plan. Next, go to the Lord in prayer. Ask him to guide you and your group. The Holy Spirit will direct you. For example, in one inner city school a group of students that loved reading decided to share their passion with less fortunate girls and boys. As a result, they started a book drive and donated hundreds of books to children in Georgia's Foster Care System.

In the event, your girls do not have any ideas of their own, several suggestions appear later in the chapter that you can present to your group. Remember it will be critical that your group buys into the ideas. You will need their full support and cooperation if the project is going to be truly successful. Once you have selected a project, get the whole community involved. You can …

- Acquire free public service announcements on local television and radio programs.
- Run advertisements in the local paper.
- Create flyers and distribute them to local churches and other community organizations.
- Write to your local government officials, the mayor, governor, senators, etc. and solicit their involvement in your project.
- Request support from corporations and small businesses in your area.

ECHOES
Making Something Out of Nothing
Ask each girl if she has a penny? Have one girl collect all of the pennies and then count them. Now ask each girl if they have a nickel? dime? quarter? dollar? Collect the nickels and total the amount. Next do this for the dimes, quarters and then finally dollars. This illustrates the point that as individuals we may not have much, but as a collective body we have much more. Now ask the girls if you can keep the pennies and nickels and make a donation to the charity of their choice - The United Way, a homeless shelter, a group home, children's hospital, a hospice, the possibilities are endless. You would be surprised at how far a little money can go. Watch as the girls are mesmerized by the power of multiplicity.

We worked in a school that sat in the middle of an inner-city public housing project. At this school a group of GEMMS started a service project. Most people wrote them off and assumed they did not have anything to give to anyone else because many of them were extremely economically disadvantaged themselves. The girl's met twice a month during the school year. They decided to donate a quarter each meeting. At some meetings everyone didn't have anything to give but as the year progressed some gave more than the quarter. By the end of the school year they had collected about three hundred dollars. They bought toothpaste, toothbrushes, soap, deodorant, body powder and lotion for homeless men and women and donated it to the homeless shelter across the street from the school. The girls had a great sense of pride and accomplishment as they presented the items to the shelter residents. The heartfelt thank you and tears from the residents meant a great deal to the girls. The experience moved the girls tremendously; as a result, they decided to make donations to the shelter on a regular basis and the next year they donated fifty cents per week and also asked others to make donations. Before long every teacher in the school either donated money or products. The principal, family members and churches got involved. What a powerful testimony! God will multiply and increase what you begin in faith in ways that you can never imagine. Step boldly; the world is waiting for your mission. Never forget that even one person can make a difference, undoubtedly a group can make an astonishing impact.

The story of the widow's mite comes to mind. (Luke 21: 1-4, Mark 12: 41 – 44) The widow gave all she had. These girls didn't have much but they gave all they had. They started a culture of giving in the school and set the example for the adults to follow. Jesus wants us to give, boldly and with a loving spirit. Just imagine what you can do through the power of giving.

POSSIBLE COMMUNITY SERVICE PROJECTS

These are only suggestions and starting points for conversation. Your project should be based on the needs of your community and the interests of your group.

- Sponsor a coat, clothing or shoe drive. Ask for gently worn or new items. Donate these items to local shelters, group homes or children in foster care.

- Organize a food drive. Collect canned goods and nonperishable items. Make donations to food banks, homeless shelters or needy families in your community.

- Have a community clean up day. Select a neighborhood park, school or street and simply pick up trash. You may go a step further: plan and plant a community garden and trees. Solicit donations from stores like Home Depot and Lowes for flowers, plants and gardening tools.

- Adopt a grandma/grandpa. Visit a senior citizens facility and volunteer to play and organize games, read books, sing or conduct other activities with residents.

- Become a reading buddy. Volunteer to read to kids in a hospital or children's shelter.

- Create cards for special occasions, birthdays, Christmas, Thanksgiving and give the cards to people at hospitals, prisons and/or shelters.

- Collect new books and donate books to children in the foster care system or to a children's shelter.

- Collect personal hygiene items, soap, deodorant, toothpaste, toothbrushes, etc. and give these items to women, men and youth in prison, and shelters. You may even place items in decorated shoeboxes for individuals with printed messages and bible verses.

- Help build a Habitat for Humanity house.

- Donate money collected to the United Negro College Fund, UNICEF, American Red Cross, CARE or other charitable organization.

- Set up a scholarship fund in the name of your group and set criteria for giving the money away

Give the money to a high school senior in your group. This money may help a girl buy books, pay room and board or other expenses related to going to college. [Note: In some states you may be required to be a legal nonprofit entity to collect and disperse funds for scholarships. Please check your state's laws.]

• Create and decorate a baby basket. Collect baby bottles, powder, wipes, and diapers. Place the items in the baskets and donate them to a women and children's shelter or crisis pregnancy centers in your area.

MILESTONES

Have the girls reflect on the scripture, Acts 20:35. Ask them to write about what it is they think that God would have them to do. Tell them to explain how it would be more blessed to give than to receive.

MAGNET

Parents can be invited to participate in community service projects. Getting parents involved will take your projects to a higher level. You can even use parent volunteers to help coordinate and execute your community service projects. On the other hand, some of your parents may need assistance themselves. Poll your parents. If there are needs create projects to meet their needs.

Pearls for Parents

- The best thing you can do is to lead by example. Let your actions speak loudly.

- Join your daughter in completing a community service project.

- Allow your daughter to help you prepare and deliver food for a sick family, church or community member.

- Always display a caring and selfless attitude.

- If possible make a family donation to the charity of your choice.

- Work as a family in a food pantry, homeless shelter or other mission project.

- Become an active volunteer in the organization of your choice.

- Do random acts of kindness on a daily basis: hold the door open for the person behind you; help someone struggling in the store.

- Say good morning to a stranger every day.

- Give one of your smiles to everyone you come in contact with every single day.

SANCTUARY

Have a reflective discussion. Girls should reflect on the service project you are working on and answer these questions: What did you learn? What skills did you gain? How did you help? How does it make you feel to know that you have done something to help someone else? What more can you do in the future? How can we involve others?

Prayer

Lord, thank you for blessing us. Please help us to bless someone else. Allow us to use the gifts and talents that you have given us to help others. Enable us to identify needs in our community, energize us to meet those needs and strengthen us. In the name of Jesus we pray.
Amen.

Additional Precious Jewel
   "I can do everything through Him who gives me strength." Philippians 4:13 (NASB)

MILESTONES

Precious Jewel

"In everything I did, I showed you that by this kind of hard work we must help the weak, remembering the words the Lord Jesus himself said, 'It is more blessed to give than to receive.'" Acts 20:35

Reflect on the scriptures, Phillipians 4:13 and Acts 20:35. Write about what it is that God would have you do for others. Explain how it would be more blessed to give than to receive.

CHAPTER 7
Keeping It Pure
Sexual Abstinence & Healthy Dating

PRECIOUS JEWEL

"Flee from sexual immorality. All other sins a man commits are outside his body, but he who sins sexually sins against his own body. Do you know that your body is a temple of the Holy Spirit, who is in you, whom you have received from God? You are not your own; you were bought at a price. Therefore honor God with your body."
1 Corinthians 6:18 – 20

"The commitment to live a life of sexual purity is easy to make and keep once you realize just how special you are."
– Michelle Easley

GATEWAY

The crisis in our communities is real. Babies are having babies, girls are being infected with HIV at alarmingly high rates, and young ladies are becoming sexually active before they turn thirteen. Young people are engaging in risky, sexual behavior. Some say the lyrics in the music; the images on the videos, and the dialogue and content matter of prime time television encourage this type of reckless behavior. Then there are those who believe that the actions of celebrities, professional athletes, and even elected officials lead our young people down a path of sexual impurity. Still others think many parents are a part of the problem. While we, the adults of the world, are arguing about the reasons our girls are lost, they are continuing to engage in behaviors that put them at extreme risk. Let's stop blaming others and focus on solving the problem. We urge you to begin to challenge your girls to reject the world's view of sex and sexuality. Today commit to empowering them to make different choices; to choose to remain pure, to treat their bodies as temples of the Holy Spirit.

DID YOU KNOW… FACTS TO SHOUT OUT

Three in ten girls become pregnant at least once before age 20 – over 750,000 teen pregnancies annually. [5] Eight in ten teen pregnancies are not planned. [6] Among Hispanics, the fastest growing ethnic group in the nation, teen birth rates are going down much slower than that for other ethnic groups. Hispanics now have the highest teen birth rate nationally; more than 51% get pregnant by the age of twenty. [7] Forty percent of mothers who have a child before they turn 18 never graduate from high school compared with about three quarters of young women who wait until they are 20 or 21. [8]

As discussed earlier in the chapter on School Success, you know that dropping out of school hurts a young woman's ability to have a bright future. Teens that have babies are more likely to need public assistance – welfare, food stamps and public housing. Unmarried teens that have not received a high school diploma or a GED are more likely to raise their child in poverty. [9]

Nationally the rate for pregnancy among teens aged 15–19 decreased 36% between 1990 and 2002. [10] The news sounds good, but in reality even one teen pregnancy is one too many. It's very clear that teen pregnancy can significantly reduce a young woman's chances of being successful. We have much work to do.

Now let's look at the other side of the coin. Sexual activity puts our girls at risk of contracting AIDS and other sexually transmitted diseases. The risk is even greater for youth of minority races and ethnicities. African Americans were disproportionately affected by HIV infection; accounting for 55% of all HIV infections reported among persons aged 13–24 according to the CDC's HIV Prevention in the Third Decade. [11] In 2004, approximately 7,761 young people were living with AIDS, a 42% increase since 2000 according to the CDC HIV/AIDS Surveillance Report 2004. [12] Since the start of the AIDS Epidemic, approximately 40,059 youth in the US received a diagnosis of AIDS, and about 10,129 young people have died from AIDS. [13]

"Young women, especially those of minority races or ethnicities are increasingly at risk for HIV infection through heterosexual contact. According to data from a CDC study HIV prevalence among disadvantaged youth during the early to mid 1990s, the rate of HIV prevalence among young women aged 16–21 was 50% higher than the rate among young men in that age group. African American women in this study group were 7 times as likely as white women and 8 times as likely as Hispanic women to be HIV-positive." [14] Sexually transmitted diseases increase a young woman's likelihood of acquiring or transmitting HIV. Some of the highest STD rates in the country are among young people, especially young people of minority races. [15] Gonorrhea rates in 2004 were highest among African Americans aged 15–24, in 2004, African American women aged 15–19 had gonorrhea at a rate of 2790.5 cases per 100,000 females. [16] This rate was 14 times greater than the 2004 rate among white females of similar age. [17]

The School Health Policies and Program Study (SHPPS), a national survey conducted among schools, found that among teachers required to teach health education, elementary school teachers taught STD prevention an average of one hour per school year; middle/junior high school teachers 2 hours and senior high school teachers 3 hours. [18] We can't expect the school to do the job of arming our girls with the information they need. STDs are a monumental public health challenge in the United States. While substantial progress has been made in preventing, diagnosing, and treating certain STDs in recent years, the CDC estimates that 19 million new infections occur each year, almost half of them among young people ages 15 to 24. [19]

We can't just shake our heads and say, "What a shame! Didn't your mother teach you any better?" We must carry this burden. It is imperative if we are to save our girls. We must empower them to make different choices. It's a fact; abstinence is the only method that is 100% effective against contracting AIDS and other sexually transmitted diseases and in preventing teenage pregnancy. We are going to have to move past our comfort zones and have open, frank dialogue with these young ladies. Gone are the days of sugar coating and dancing around the real issues. Here's how you can get the conversation going.

MIXER

Baby Mama

Invite young mothers to come in and talk to the group about the challenges they face on a day-to-day basis, particularly the struggles they face trying to finish high school, work, live and raise a baby. Ask your invited guest to be very honest with your group. Allow time for questions and answers.

ECHOES

Pledge of Purity Ceremony

Have each girl sign a Pledge of Purity located at the end of this chapter. This should be strictly voluntary. Stress the fact that even though some girls may have already engaged in sex, it's never too late to make a change. Present each girl with some symbol that physically represents the commitment she is making. Suggestions include the silicone wristband with "Purity" written on it, purity rings or bracelets. These are available at local Christian stores or from online Christian retailers.

Have each girl read her pledge aloud.

Purity Bracelet

You may choose to have the girls create their own purity bracelet. This is a very simple, inexpensive craft.

- You will need to purchase black leather cording and alphabet beads. You may decide to use gemstone beads perhaps, clear, white or pink and create a pattern to represent purity. If you use the alphabet beads, use the letters to spell out the word "purity." These items can be found at local craft stores.
- You simply string the beads on the leather cord.
- Knot the cord in place on the wrist of each girl.

Pink is the most rare and expensive diamond. If you elect to use pink beads tell the girls that the pink represents them - unique, rare and priceless. Of course, the white or clear represents their commitment to being pure.

Will simply wearing a purity bracelet or reciting a purity pledge change the behavior of the girls? Will these simple acts cause them to abstain from sex? Probably not, but the whole point of this exercise is to raise their level of consciousness. You want to make the girls think differently, to challenge the world's view of sex and sexuality. If you get the girls to even consider the possibility of abstaining from sex you have accomplished much.

HEALTHY DATING: A DISCUSSION

What's the perfect date? You will need to lead your girls in discussion and cover the following points. Remember honest, frank discussion is your main objective. Make sure the girls feel free to discuss what is really on their minds without fear of judgment and ridicule.

What's a perfect date? The perfect date is a healthy date. Your parents know, approve and give you permission to date. There is no sneaking, hiding or being dishonest. You and your date should discuss and agree on where the date will take place and what you will do. If his idea of fun is going riding on a motorcycle but you're afraid to ride one, you should not feel pressured to ride. Your date should respect you as a person. You should be able to talk to your date and not feel threatened in any way. Your date should bring you home at the time you agreed on with your parents. This means if you are told to be home by 11:00 p.m., your date isn't asking you to hang out after midnight.

How rough is too rough? A healthy date is not violent or overly aggressive. He should not show signs of jealously or physical dominance. It's not cute for a guy to play or pretend fight with you. That is choking you around the neck, hitting or pushing you or trying to knock you down. He should not be physically, emotionally, mentally or sexually abusive. A date does not mean ownership. It's a way to begin a friendship. Your date should never force you to use drugs or alcohol or to have sex. As a matter of fact, your date should not force you to do anything you don't want to do.

Is name calling a sign? You should not, under any circumstances, accept behavior from your date that makes you feel less than a person, puts you down, criticizes you or makes you feel crazy. Your date should not call you names like, fat, crazy, ho, or bitch. Some rap music glamorizes the terms, but make no mistake about it the words are negative, hateful and hurtful. Don't allow someone to label you. Always demand to be treated with respect and dignity. If your date tries to belittle your morals, Christian values and beliefs then reconsider your decision to be involved with him.

DATING DOS & DON'TS

Consider these dos & don'ts of dating.

- Be aware of your surroundings on a date. Don't agree to park at the end of a dimly lit, deserted street or walk through an empty park. You and your date could become victims of a violent crime.

- Keep yourself safe.

CYBER SAFETY & ONLINE DATING OR SOCIALIZING

If you explore the Internet for social interactions or just to hang out and have fun, keep safety foremost in your mind.

- Never give out personal information like your phone number or address.

- Don't send pictures of yourself, especially pictures showing yourself in revealing clothing or partially nude.

- Don't participate in conversations online that are sexual in nature. There are many predators lurking online just waiting for their next victim.

- If you chat online with strangers keep your guard up. Many use the Internet as a means of stealing a person's identity.

- Don't ever give out personal information about yourself or family members like your name, date of birth, social security number, or address. This information can be used to open credit cards, take out loans and even commit crimes. Guard your personal information closely.

- **Never** agree to meet someone in person that you have only communicated with online.

ONE LAST WARNING: DATE RAPE DRUGS

Keep in mind that date rape drugs do exist. **Rohypnol,** commonly know as **Roofies** are small, white, round tablets. These are odorless, tasteless pills that can be dissolved in drinks and are hard to detect. Some use them to make women more submissive. Women have been raped after having ingested the drugs. They reported having memory loss and a decrease in resistance. **Gamma Hydroxybutyrate** or **GHB** is a sedative, also known as **Liquid Ecstasy.** This drug can be a grainy white powder or clear liquid. Women stated the drug made them feel like they had too much alcohol to drink. They said they felt as though they were functioning in a state of confusion and had little control over their own bodies.

RESOURCE
National Domestic Violence Hotline
1.800.799.SAFE

MILESTONES

Have each girl assume the role of advice columnist. They will respond to the letters located at the end of the chapter. Tell the girls to keep the precious jewel, scriptural reference of 1 Corinthians 6:18 – 20, in mind when answering the questions. Additionally, write about how the scripture should influence you to strive to be sexually pure.

MAGNET

Invite parents to your meeting. Have them create a "Mom's Memo". This is simply a letter from the mother to the daughter about what her expectations are. The mothers may include such topics as curfews, acceptable places to go on a date and what to do in case of an emergency.

Pearls for Parents

1. Set boundaries for your daughter, such as, no clubs, alcohol, or sex.

2. Discuss what she's wearing. Is it appropriate? Is it too low cut? Too tight? Revealing?

3. Know where she is, whom she is with and what she is doing. [You may not actually know what she is doing, but encourage her to tell you the plan: going skating, to the movies, out to eat, etc.]

4. Don't be afraid to tell your daughter NO! If her date looks too old or she says something that doesn't make sense, tell her NO!

5. Set a curfew.

6. Encourage open and honest communication – call if you're late, ask for help if you need it even if it's a difficult situation.

7. Tell you daughter not to drink and drive or ever get in the car where the driver is drunk or under the influence of drugs.

8. Let your daughter know that you want her to say no to sex, drugs and alcohol.

9. Tell you daughter you love her unconditionally.

10. Expect your daughter to make mistakes, learn from them and move on.

11. Look over your daughter's shoulder while she is on the Internet.

12. If your daughter has a personal webpage on any of the popular social networking sites view her home page. Make her take down pages that contain inappropriate pictures, poses, words, etc.

SANCTUARY

Form a prayer circle. Ask for prayer requests. Lead the group in prayer.

Dear God,
Give me the strength to stay pure in your sight. Help me to stay focused on my goals and save my purity for a loving, committed marriage relationship. Help me to stay safe in my dating relationships. Give me the strength and courage to leave unhealthy, negative dates and the wisdom to recognize them. Help me to be a true friend to my sisters, encouraging them to live a life of purity. Surround me with your love, grace and mercy. In Jesus name I pray.
Amen

GEMMS PLEDGE OF PURITY

I _____ (name) promise to live a pure life. I will treat my body as a temple of the Holy Spirit. I promise not to engage in sexual activity until I am married. I will help my sisters as they work to keep this pledge. I know this may be difficult at times so I will seek God first and pray daily. I promise to live a life free from drugs, alcohol and sex. I know that even if I make a mistake God's love, mercy and grace will sustain me. I will be forgiven and I can start anew.

_____   _____

Signature   Date

ADVICE COLUMN

Dear GEMMS:
I have been dating my boyfriend for 2 months. We have gone to the movies, skating and the park; however, he is beginning to pressure me to have sex. I like him. He's a star football player, respected by all the teachers at school and he is extremely cute, in other words he has it going on. I don't want to loose him. How do I keep him if I don't have sex? What do I do?

Love,
Confused

Dear GEMMS:
My boyfriend and I have been dating for several months. Lately, he has started to push me, and pretend he's choking me. My mother and even my friends have said they have noticed him being too rough with me. He says he is just playing but I really don't like it. I am kind of afraid. What should I do? Is it okay for him to play with me this way?

Luv,
Tired of being pushed on

MILESTONES

Precious Jewel

"Flee from sexual immorality. All other sins a man commits are outside his body, but he who sins sexually sins against his own body. Do you know that your body is a temple of the Holy Spirit, who is in you, whom you have received from God? You are not your own; you were bought at a price. Therefore honor God with your body."
1 Corinthians 6:18 – 20

Reflect on the Precious Jewel above; write about how this should influence you as you strive to be sexually pure. Then assume the role of advice columnist and respond to a "Dear GEMMs" letter.

◆
CHAPTER 8
You Got Issues
Living Peacefully In A Violent World

PRECIOUS JEWEL

"Turn from evil and do good; seek peace and pursue it."
Psalms 34:14

"Love is the only force capable of transforming an enemy into a friend."
– Martin Luther King, Jr.

GATEWAY

All anyone has to do is turn on the news or open a newspaper to see that we all live with extraordinary amounts of violence. Children, youth, teens and young adults kill one another over trivial matters. An argument in a mall about an ex-girlfriend can spill over to a gunfight in a parking lot with a tragic ending. A little girl playing at her computer in her apartment looses her life after someone outside her window decides to settle a score with a gun. Too many mothers, fathers, sisters and cousins have had to shed far too many tears over the open graves and caskets of loved ones lost to senseless violence. It's a huge problem. Many comment that the violence in our society is so far out of control there's absolutely nothing any person, group, politician, social organization or church can do about it. Gangs have taken over our schools, recruiting members as early as elementary school. Girls are not immune.

Let's try this; instead of focusing on the problem we'll start to work on the solution. We believe the single most effective book on nonviolence is *The Holy Bible.* Most kids aren't going to just sit around and read the bible and glean its message of nonviolence, but that's where you come in. You will extract the verses and begin to plant the seeds of peace, love and hope into the minds, hearts and souls of the GEMMS you work with. Imagine this… if you reach just one girl and she really gets the message she can go to her school and back into her community and spread the word to one of her friends and that friend can tell another friend and so on and so forth. The power of one is far greater than you think. Now imagine you work with a group of twenty, thirty, forty or even a hundred girls, the results are multiplied. Believe in the impossible and watch as the garden of peace and love grow in your community, city, state, nation and world.

This is difficult work, but it can be done. Progress may not be evident to you at all. Trust that with God changes are happening. You must remain strong and committed. We once worked with a group of young ladies that had spent time incarcerated. They were accustomed to fighting in the street in front of the fast food restaurant in their neighborhood. We dialogued with them and discovered that they usually were fighting over a guy. We encouraged them to turn the other cheek, walk away or avoid the restaurant all together. At first they literally called us names and told us they had to save face by fighting in the neighborhood. They said the thought of walking away from a fight was completely ridiculous. As a matter of fact, many of the girls had gone to the juvenile detention center for fighting with razors in public. After many weeks of conversation and activities one of the most popular girls, Angie*, announced to the group that she would try what we said just once and report back on how things went. We really didn't believe her but prayed that evening and anxiously awaited her return. The next week came, and Angie didn't show up. She came back to the group meeting a few weeks later and told us that she walked away from a fight. She said she stepped toward the girl's face and instead of hitting her; she invited her to one of our group meetings. She said everyone in the parking lot called her a punk, a wimp and other derogatory names. Angie ignored them and walked away. Angie now goes straight home from school and avoids the fast food restaurant's parking lot altogether. We never would have believed Angie would do this, but she did. God is awesome!
(*Name was changed to ensure anonymity.)

MIXER
You say you got DRAMA?
Ask each girl to write down one problem she is presently experiencing. This should be private; the girls do not have to record their names on the paper. Collect all the papers and read the drama notes aloud. Check to see if any one issue seems to be recurring. If so, you may chose to focus your discussion on this topic. Next, ask the girls to count off, for example from 1 – 5. Assign one adult facilitator to each number. Move each group of girls to a different area and discuss the issues they wrote about on the paper. Set ground rules in the large group setting before you break into the smaller groups.
Some suggested rules:

1. Girls may not talk about anyone by name.

2. No one should speak while someone else is talking.

3. All girls must be respectful and loving. No one should be ridiculed or judged for what they say.

4. All comments made must remain in the meeting room. The girls shouldn't go back and repeat what was said to friends at school or in their neighborhood.

ECHOES
Pass the Daisy – Discussion Activity
   • Reiterate the rules in the small group.

- Girls should read aloud the *Confidentiality Pledge.*

- Let everyone know that all groups will reconvene in a set period of time to report back to the large group. You may set aside twenty-five minutes of small group discussion and fifteen minutes for the whole group. Actually give the girls a specific time to meet back with the group.

- Assign three jobs:
  Recorder – take notes
  Reporter – report back to the large group
  Timekeeper – notify the group when ten minutes remains and when time is up.

- Each group will discuss a topic from the *You Say You Got Drama* activity. In the unlikely event your group does not come up with any topics sample topics are included at the end of the chapter.

- Give the Daisy, any artificial flower will do, to a girl and begin to chat. Set a time limit, i.e. each girl will have three minutes to talk. Have the timekeeper call time in three minutes. The girl will pass the daisy to the next girl that will talk. The daisy doesn't have to be passed in order, just make sure that everyone that wishes to speak has an opportunity to do so. Remember the girl must be holding the daisy in order to speak. After everyone has spoken, give the daisy to the reporter. You may wish to use a discussion guide sheet such as the one that appears at the end of the chapter. If you use the discussion guide, make sure the recorder completes the sheet as the group talks.

- When the large group reassembles allow each group to share what they discussed and learned, and if they came up with any solutions to problems.

This activity was done with a group of girls in a community where gang violence was rampant. Consequently, everyone chose to discuss gangs. They wanted to talk about how pressured they felt to become part of gangs at school. They described the brutal physical initiations that included beatings, burnings and forced sex. They spoke of how they avoided using the restroom at school for fear of being sexually and physically assaulted. The girls felt helpless and powerless to escape or seek help. The ensuing conversations were riveting. At the end of the sessions the girls felt relief in having been able to verbalize their concerns. After hearing these horrific accounts we spoke with the community resource officer. As a result, a community leader was contacted. They agreed to institute a gang deterrent program in the school.

*Note: if serious, personal issues, such as abuse and neglect arise during the discussion, you may be required by law to involve the proper authorities. Pregnancy, alcohol and drug abuse may require that you involve parents, caretakers or other adults. This can potentially be a very delicate area and may require professional intervention.

Actin' Out
Have the girls count off by fours. Have all the number ones come together, number twos, etc. Have each group get a role-play card. The girls should create a skit to dramatize their solution to the problem presented on the role-play card. Each group should read their card aloud to the group. Role-play cards are

located at the end of the chapter.

Precious Jewels Probe
Read aloud the additional Precious Jewels located at the end of the chapter. Ask each girl to select at least two scriptures and tell how the scriptures can help them to live a life free of violence and conflict.

MILESTONES
Have the girls write reflectively. They may wish to consider the following: Could you use the scriptures presented to help you avoid conflict? Could sharing the scripture, Psalms 34:14, help you or someone you know? Explain.

MAGNET
Have a special session to include parents. During the session repeat the activities, *Pass the Daisy* and *You Say You Got Drama.*

Pearls for Parents

• Have open, honest discussions with you daughter on a regular basis.

• Encourage your daughter to speak freely with you, even about difficult topics.

• Seek the help of a professional counselor if your daughter is experiencing serious problems.

• Encourage your daughter to tell you if she feels she is being bullied or threatened at school or in the neighborhood.

• Teach your daughter how to resolve arguments and misunderstandings without violence and aggression.

• Do not spread gossip.

• Respect others and value diversity.

• Set a good example. Be positive and peaceful!

SANCTUARY

Have the girls form a prayer circle. Accept prayer requests. An adult facilitator and a girl can lead the prayer. Emphasize to the girls the importance of prayer and bible study. Let them know that a faith-filled walk with God will help them as they face the many issues that life may bring their way. This will also help them make wise choices and seek to obtain peaceful solutions to all problems and conflicts.

Prayer

Dear God,
Please help us as we journey though life. Many of us face issues on a daily basis. Whether they are financial, physical, emotional or personal help us to realize that with and through you all things are possible. Increase our faith, renew our strength. Enable us to walk away from fights and arguments. Help us to love our enemies. Empower us to be agents of change bringing peace to every aspect of our world. Protect us Lord. We ask these blessings in the name of your son Jesus.
Amen

ADDITIONAL PRECIOUS JEWELS

"May the God of hope fill you with all joy and peace as you trust in him, so that you may overflow with hope by the power of the Holy Spirit." Romans 15:13

"But the fruit of the Spirit is love, joy, peace, patience, kindness, goodness, faithfulness, gentleness and self-control." Galatians 5: 22

"A fool gives full vent to his anger, but a wise man keeps himself under control." Proverbs 29:11

"Without wood a fire goes out; without gossip a quarrel dies down." Proverbs 26:20

"Do not say, "I'll pay you back for this wrong." Wait for the Lord and he will deliver you." Proverbs 20:22

"Hatred stirs up dissension but love covers over all wrongs." Proverbs 10:12

"A gentle answer turns away wrath, but a harsh word stirs up anger." Proverbs 15:1

"You have heard that it was said, 'Love your neighbor and hate your enemy' But I tell you: Love your enemies and pray for those who persecute you, that you may be sons of your Father in heaven. He causes his sun to rise on the evil and the good, and sends rain on the righteous and the unrighteous." Matthew 5: 43 – 45

"But I tell you who hear me: Love your enemies, do good to those who hate you, bless those who curse you, pray for those who mistreat you. If someone strikes you on one cheek, turn to him the other also. If someone takes your cloak, do not stop him from taking your tunic. Give to everyone who asks you, and if anyone takes what belongs to you, do not demand it back. Do to others as you would have them do to you." Luke 6:27 – 31

"Blessed are the peacemakers, for they will be called sons of God." Matthew 5: 9

YOU GOT ISSUES
LIVING PEACEFULLY IN A VIOLENT WORLD

Sample Topics

Bullying

Gangs

Sex

Alcohol

Drugs

Curfews

Parents

Friends

Teachers

Dating

School

Church

Homework

PASS THE DAISY

Record names	
Group Name:	
Member's names:	
Reporter:	
Recorder:	
Time keeper:	

Create a question based on your topic.

Main points discussed (list 3 main points)

State the problem / give examples or specifics

State the solution
Other comments

ROLE-PLAY CARDS

CUT ALONG DOTTED LINES

ROLE-PLAY #1

Discuss the situation and then act it out. Act out what you think you should do in each situation. Think about the consequences of your actions and be prepared to discuss them with the group.

You and your friends are walking home from school. One of your friends tells you that she doesn't like one particular girl walking in the group. She starts to call her names and then begins to push her. She encourages you to join in. What do you do?

ROLE-PLAY #2

Discuss the situation and then act it out. Act out what you think you should do in each situation. Think about the consequences of your actions and be prepared to discuss them with the group.

Everyday at school a girl calls you names and embarrasses you in class. She really goes out of her way to humiliate you. Your best friend tells you that you should beat her up after P.E. class. What should you do?

ROLE-PLAY #3

Discuss the situation and then act it out. Act out what you think you should do in each situation. Think about the consequences of your actions and be prepared to discuss them with the group.

A kid in your class brings a gun to school. He says he tired of everyone picking on him. He shows you the gun and tells you not to tell anyone, especially a teacher. What do you do?

ROLE-PLAY #4

Discuss the situation and then act it out. Act out what you think you should do in each situation. Think about the consequences of your actions and be prepared to discuss them with the group.

A student sends a threatening email and several threatening text messages to one of the most popular girls at school. In the message she tells her that she will wait for her after school, beat her up and then take her purse, book bag and shoes. She tells you to send the same message also because it's only a joke. What do you do?

MILESTONES

Precious Jewel

"Turn from evil and do good; seek peace and pursue it." Psalms 34:14

Reflect on the Precious Jewel printed above and the other Precious Jewels presented this session; write about how could you use these scriptures to help you avoid conflict?

◆
CHAPTER 9
Extensions
Bonding Through Books

Books offer us an inexpensive way of experiencing new places and adventures. Through books one can travel to different places, and times, and meet people from other cultures. We can escape our own realities; learn valuable lessons and understand the mistakes others have made. Harness the power of books and form a book club. You can even invite the parents to join in your group. A mother-daughter book club is an excellent way to open dialogue about difficult topics such as teen sex, drug and alcohol use.

Book clubs have many positive benefits. Students that read more tend to score higher on standardized assessments. Reading helps one increase their vocabulary and overall comprehension skills. Girls may improve their ability to critically analyze what they have read. Reading exposes them to new ideas, concepts and cultures. It also helps students to become better writers. Most importantly, it will help your girls develop and maintain a lifelong love of reading.

It's always a good idea to let your girls chose the book they would like to read. Some people may worry about the varying reading levels present in the group. You may have strong and weak readers. More than likely a wide range of reading abilities will be present. In an effort to address this you can pair the girls up or try to select materials that can be enjoyed by all. Whatever you do, don't get hung up on this point. If you have to read aloud to the girls and tell them to follow along with you, do that. Ideally, you would want to read books that provide positive messages or provoke deep, thoughtful discussions. Many people think that fiction titles are the best types of books to read with young people but nonfiction and biographies can be just as powerful.

You can ask the girls to buy their own books, check them out from the public library or have some type of fundraiser to raise money to purchase books for all of the girls. Ask church and community members to donate funds to purchase books. A book purchase is an investment in the future. It is money well spent.

A short list of recommended titles is:

Before the Moon Rises by Michelle Easley

The Payton Skyy Series by Stephanie Perry Moore

The Baptism by Shelia P. Moses

Life Lessons for My Sisters by Natasha Munson

Yolanda's Genius by Carol Fenner

Double Dutch by Sharon Draper

The Skin I'm In by Sharon Flake

Kira Kira by Cynthia Kadohota

Heaven by Angela Johnson

Esperanza Rising by Pam Munoz Ryan

An Unlikely Friendship: A Novel of Mary Todd Lincoln and Elizabeth Keckley by Ann Rinaldi

Dignifying Science: Stories About Women Scientist by Jim OHaviani

Nobody Owns the Sky: The Story of Brave Bessie Coleman by Reeve Lindbergh

The Voice that Challenged a Nation: Marian Anderson and the Struggle for Equal Rights by Russell Freedman

Generally, you will want to assign specific pages or chapters for the girls to read before each meeting. You should have guided discussion questions for the chapters you are reading. Give the questions to the girls before they begin to read the assigned pages. You may even want to allow time for the girls to read a few pages aloud at the designated meetings. You may elect to have the book club meeting as a part of your regularly scheduled meeting or have it on another day. Once you begin the book it is important to maintain a regular, consistent schedule to keep the girls interested and on track. It is a good idea not to allow too much time to pass between meetings. For example, meet at least once every other week to discuss the book. Most importantly, finish the book. Some girls have never read an entire book from cover to cover, do not allow them to tell you, "I'm bored", "I don't like this book", "I'm tired of reading this" or "Can we read something else now?" Force them to stick with the book. This is the only way that they can truly experience the book.

RESPONSE ACTIVITIES

In addition to discussion questions you may want to complete other response activities after you read.

• Create a new ending to the story. Have the girls write an alternate ending to a book they have read and share it with the group.

• Make a book cover. Have the girls design a book cover for the book. Make sure they include detailed illustrations that reflect the setting, characters and major theme of the book and include the title and author of the book. On the opposite side of the paper they can write a brief summary of the book.

• Create a play based on a book. Have the girls act out the play. Invite their parents, family and friends to see the show.

- Have the girls research the author and write or email the author questions about the book. Do an author study: Compile the question and answers in a scrapbook. Invite the author to a meeting for book discussion. Make this a big event, invite community members and serve refreshments.

- Have girls create a story map – in which they diagram the characters, setting, problems and solutions. This is a visual map of the story. A story map can be found at the end of the chapter.

- Have the girls make a collage that represents images taken from the book. The pictures could represent the main characters or overall theme of the book read.

- Write a book review. They would need to provide a brief summary of the book, include their opinion of the book. Tell whether or not they would recommend it to a friend and gives reasons to support their recommendation.

- Take a field trip that relates to the book in some way. A group of girls we worked with read a book that was set during the time of Jim Crow laws. We took a field trip to the Civil Rights Institute in Birmingham, Alabama. This experience brought the book to life and added depth to our reading experience.

- Have a special guest come in and talk about a subject related to the book. If you read a book about a troubled teen you may invite a police officer, judge or social worker in to talk about the real life consequences of making poor decisions.

- Integrate technology – have students create a PowerPoint® about the book or create a webpage. Relax, even if you're not tech savvy usually there is a girl in the group that would be more than willing to take the lead on this type of project. Consider publishing your web page on the World Wide Web, but be sure you have written parental permission before you do this.

- Start a blog. Have your girls create a blog on the book and invite others to join in the chat. There are many free sites that allow you to create a blog. Just Google® the word "blog" and get started. In this instance, written parental permission is necessary.

CULTURAL ENRICHMENT

There is nothing like the exposure to something new and exciting to motivate young people to achieve and dream big. If the girls have never seen a professional African American or Hispanic ballerina, they may think that these ballerinas only exist within the pages of a story book. Many young people have never heard the thunder of the tympanis at the symphony or seen the vibrant colors of a full theatrical production on stage. Many young ladies have never experienced events that you take for granted. Consider organizing the following trips.

- See a gospel concert

- Attend a stage play

- Visit a symphony performance

- Visit a local museum or art gallery
- Organize a tour of colleges and universities in your area
- Dine at a five star restaurant
- Tour a local business

If you're thinking you don't have the money, or your girls can't afford to pay, ask community members, churches or corporations to sponsor you. Contact the places you plan to visit directly and ask for reduced or free admission. You can even call on elected officials in your area. Elected officials generally have connections with lots of different people and may be able to put you in touch with persons or organizations that can help. Remember to be positive and persistent. Usually you will find someone that is willing to help youth in need. Local restaurants may even be able to provide your meal at a discounted rate or for free. Call in advance and speak with the establishment's manager or owner. A sample field trip letter and permission form has been included at the end of this chapter.

SUGGESTED CULMINATING ACTIVITY

Mother & Daughter Tea

As a celebration of a successful year have a mother/daughter tea. This event can be planned very simply or it can be extravagant; whatever your budget allows. The purpose of the Mother/Daughter Tea is to simply honor the girls you have been working with. During this event you can also pay tribute to the mothers. If a girl's mother cannot participate you can step in to be her mother for the day. She may also consider inviting her favorite teacher, a community or church member, or another relative to stand in her mother's place.

Form the following committees, assign girls and parent volunteers to work on each:
Invitation
Program
Decorations
Refreshments
Souvenirs

The invitation committee will actually create the invitation and compose a list of guests. You may wish to mail the invitations or send them home with the girls. Don't forget to invite all those who have worked with you throughout the year. You can acknowledge them during your program. If you have any sponsors, definitely add them to your invitation list. Invite the girl's teachers from school, the school's principal, community members and church members. Don't forget the elected officials that provided assistance to you throughout the year.

The program committee will need to decide who will extend greetings, read the group's purpose, serve as Mistress of Ceremonies, and hostesses. This committee will also need to make other decisions about music, what type will be played, live or recorded, gospel, jazz or classical, the order of the program and the like. You may also wish to have your girls create a talent showcase featuring dance performances, singing, spoken word, instrumental performances, dramatization and/or a fashion show. You may even wish to have a guest speaker. This could be a beauty queen, elected official or motivational speaker. It's a nice touch to present each girl with a certificate or inexpensive trophy for her participation for the year. Present your volunteers and sponsors with tokens of appreciation. This could be a bouquet of flowers, certificate or plaque.

We once had an awesome event called "The Future on Parade," which featured girls modeling beautiful spring outfits, while the commentator announced each girl's name, the college she planned to attend, and her future professional and personal goals. All of the girls wore hats and white gloves.

The decoration committee will need to select a theme, i.e. Spring Garden. This theme should be carried out in the music, food and decorations. Your budget will be your guide, but you may wish to have fresh flowers as table decorations, chair covers, tablecloths, candles and balloons. You may elect to rent china and silverware for your affair.

The refreshment committee will decide on food and beverage items. Keep it simple and affordable but elegant and tasteful. Don't forget to relate your food table to your theme. Everyone loves cake, so get a decorated sheet cake for your desert table. This will add color to your overall food presentation. Fresh fruits and vegetables are wonderful items to present. Punch, iced tea and lemonade are perfect choices for inexpensive beverages.

Souvenirs are a perfect touch. This committee will purchase attractive, inexpensive cups and saucers. Use these to serve delicious blends of herbal teas and allow each guest to take their cup and saucer with them as a souvenir. Once we had a tea and purchased cups and saucers with beautiful flower patterns from the Goodwill and local thrift stores. This saved us a great deal of money, the girls loved drinking from the cups. You can also give each participant a small gift bag. These bags may be filled with a book mark, sample body lotions or other inexpensive toiletry items. The girls can make items such as personalized mugs, framed poems dedicated to mom, notepads or potpourri bags.

Once you have formed all of the committees and assigned tasks, give each committee a specific deadline. It is a good idea to start planning for your Mother & Daughter Tea at least four months in advance. If you need to book a room you may want to start even earlier. Above all have fun! We have included a sample program at the end of the chapter.

FIELD TRIP LETTER

Date _____

Dear Parents:

We are delighted to inform you that we will take a trip to experience

_____ on _____ [date]. We

will leave _____ [place of departure] at _____ [time] on

_____ [date] and return by _____ [time]. Please make sure your

daughter arrives on time. You must return the attached permission slip by ____

[date] if you would like for your daughter to participate. It must be filled out

completely and signed. We greatly appreciate your support.

Sincerely,

PARENT RELEASE/PERMISSION FORM - FIELD TRIP

I/we consent to (Student's Name) _____
going to (Destination) _____
on _____. Time of Departure _____ Place of
departure _____ Approximate Time of Return _____
for supervised activities, and agree to release and discharge _____,
its officers, agents, volunteers and employees, exercising reasonable care, from ___
any and all liability growing out of personal injuries and property damage resulting
or occurring during the aforementioned activity, or in transit to and from said
activity.

Dated:_____, 20_____

Parent/Guardian Signature_____

My daughter, _____ will be picked up at _____ (time)
[Please check one]
_____ by _____ (person's name) _____ (phone number)
_____ she will walk home.
_____ Other, please explain: _____

_____

_____
Parent/Guardian Signature   **Date**

RELEASE: If emergency medical treatment is required and the parents or legal guardian
cannot be reached immediately, your signature in the space provided below empowers the
_____ to send the student
(properly accompanied) for treatment to a hospital emergency room.
_____ **Parent/Guardian Signature** _____ **Date**

I can be reached on the day of the field trip at the following phone # _____.
            THIS FORM MUST BE RETURNED BY _____.

BOOK MAP

CHARACTERS	SETTING
MAJOR PROBLEM	**SOLUTION**
MAJOR PROBLEM	**SOLUTION**
WHAT I LIKED MOST ABOUT THE BOOK	**WOULD YOU RECOMMEND THIS BOOK TO A FRIEND? WHY?**

GEMMS
Mother & Daughter Tea

Welcome

GEMMS Pledge

Purpose

Musical Selection

Talent Showcase

Presentation of Awards

Acknowledgements and Thank Yous

Prayer

Refreshments are served

CHAPTER 10
Invitation To Salvation

GEMMS are invited to give their lives to Jesus Christ!

"That if you confess with your mouth, 'Jesus is Lord,' and believe in your heart that God raised him from the dead, you will be saved. For it is with your heart that you believe and are justified, and it is with your mouth that you confess and are saved."
Roman 10: 9-10

"For, 'everyone who calls on the name of the Lord will be saved.'"
Romans 10:13

"In reply Jesus declared, 'I tell you the truth, no one can see the kingdom of God unless he is born again.'"
John 3:3

"For God so loved the world, that he gave his only begotten Son, that whosoever believeth in him should not perish, but have everlasting life."
John 3:16 [King James Version]

As you have journeyed through the process of making GEMMS some of your girls may have been moved to establish a deeper relationship with God. Invite them to give their lives to Christ. As a leader you may or may not be a minister but you can still guide them in this process. Have all of the girls that decided to accept Jesus as their personal savior pray this prayer:

Dear God,
I believe that you are the God of all and that Jesus is your Holy Son. I accept you as my personal Savior. I believe that Jesus died on the cross to save me. I ask for forgiveness of my sins and direction in my life. Help me to find a church home where I can worship with other believers and feel your loving presence. Thank you for the gift of salvation. In the name of Jesus Christ,
Amen

After the girls have prayed this prayer, congratulate them for making this powerful, life-changing decision. Encourage them to find a sound, biblically based church and make efforts to change their lives one day at a time. Salvation is a way of life and not just something you do for a day. Also encourage the girls to seek counsel from genuine, mature Christians. These girls proclamation of faith can be attributed to your guidance and devotion to furthering God's kingdom. You have truly created a GEMM! Congratulations on a job well done!

WEBSITES

**Websites on the Internet are provided for our readers and do not constitute or imply endorsement of the organizations or their programs by the authors. The authors are not responsible for the content of the sites. URL addresses listed were current as of the date of publication of this book.

I LOVE ME
http://www.4girls.gov
Sponsored by the National Women's Health Information Center and the United States Department of Health and Human Services Office on Women's Health

LOOKING GOOD FEELING GREAT
http://www.mypyramid.gov
United States Department of Agriculture Food Guide Pyramid

http://www.presidentschallenge.org
Presidential Fitness Challenge

http://www.essence.com
Home of Essence Magazine

http://www.oprah.com
Home of O Magazine

GETTING WHERE I WANT TO BE
http://www.bls.gov/oco
US Department of Labor Bureau of Labor / Occupational Outlook Handbook online I'M ON THE HONOR ROLL

http://www.silentepidemic.org
Focuses on preventing dropout among high school students

http://www.dropoutprevention.org
National Dropout Prevention Center

SERVICE WITH A SMILE
http://www.habitat.org
Habitat for Humanity

http://national.unitedway.org
United Way

http://www.care.org
CARE

http://www.unicef.org
UNICEF

http://www.redcross.org
American Red Cross

http://www.uncf.org
United Negro College Fund

http://www2.oprah.com/index.jhtml
Orpah Winfrey's Philanthropy link

http://www.hoseafeedthehungry.com
Hosea Feed the Hungry and Homeless

KEEPING IT PURE
http://www.cdc.gov
Centers for Disease Control and Prevention

http://www.teenpregnancy.org
National Campaign to Prevent Teen Pregnancy

http://www.ncadv.org
The National Coalition against Domestic Violence

http://www.endabuse.org
Family Violence Prevention Fund

http://www.nrcdv.org
National Resource on Domestic Violence

YOU GOT ISSUES
http://www.usip.org
United States Institute of Peace

http://stopbullyingnow.hrsa.gov
United States Department of Health and Human Services Bullying Information

http://www.safeyouth.org/scripts/teens.asp
National Youth Violence Prevention Resource Center

http://www.sadd.org
Students Against Destructive Decisions

WORKS CITED

[1] Anorexia Nervosa and Related Eating Disorders, Inc. Statistics: How Many People Have Eating Disorders? 3 July 2007 http://www.anred.com/stats.html

[2] U.S. Department of Education, National Center for Education Statistics. (2006). (Digest of Education Statistics, 2005) (NCES 2006-030), Table 105.

[3] Dropout Rate in the United States 2005 NCES 2007-059 June 2007 Institute of Education Sciences U.S.Department of Education 30 June 2007 http://nces.ed.gov/pubs2007/dropout05

[4] Reimer, Mary & Smink, Jay. Information about the School Dropout Issue: Selected Facts & Statistics National Dropout Prevention Center Network 30 June 2007 http://www.dropoutprevention.org

[5] National Campaign to Prevent Teen Pregnancy How is the 3 in 10 Statistic Calculated? 2006. Washington DC

[6] Finer, L.B. & Henshaw, S.K. Disparities in rates of Unintended Pregnancy in the United States, 1994 and 2001. (Perspective on Sexual and Reproductive Health, 2006) 38 (2):p. 90-96.

[7] Hamilton, B.E. Martin, J.A. Ventura, S.J. Births: Preliminary Data for 2005. Health E-Stats, 2006.

[8] Hoffman, S.D. (By the Numbers; The Public Cost of Adolescent Childbearing, 2006), The National Campaign to Prevent Teen Pregnancy Washington DC.

[9] Committee on Ways and Means Democrats, Steep decline in Teen Birth Rate Significantly Responsible for Reducing Child Poverty and Single Parent Families, Committee Issue Brief, April 23, 2004. 2004 Washington DC

[10] Teen Pregnancy rates in the United States, 1972 – 2002. The National Campaign to Prevent Teen Pregnancy. 1 June 2007 http://www.teenpregnancy.org

[11] CDC. (HIV Prevention in the Third Decade). Atlanta. US Department of Health and Human Services, CDC. 2005

[12] CDC (HIV AIDS Surveillance Report 2004). Vol. 16 Atlanta: US Department of Health and Human Services CDC 2005 1 – 46.

[13] Ibid

[14] Fact Sheet: HIV/AIDS amoung Youth June 2006 25 June 2007 <http://www.cdc.gov/hiv/resources/factsheets/youth.htm>

[15] Centers for Disease Control and Prevention. (Sexually Transmitted Disease Surveillance, 2004). Atlanta, GA: US Department of Health and Human Services, September 2005.

[16] Ibid.

[17] Ibid.

[18] Fact Sheet Sexually Transmitted Diseases (STD) Prevention CDC's School Health Policies and Programs Study 2000 20 June 2007
<http://www.cdc.gov/HealthyYouth/shpps/factsheets/pdf/stdprev.pdf>

[19] Weinstock H, et al. Sexually transmitted diseases among American youth: incidence and prevalence estimates, 2000. (Perspectives on Sexual and Reproductive Health 2004):36 (1):6-10.

ACKNOWLEDGEMENTS

We first give thanks and praise to God for placing this calling on our hearts. We pay tribute to him for sustaining us and allowing us to complete this project even in the midst of personal, seemingly insurmountable, crises. His love, grace and mercy were a constant and for this we say thank you.

Thank you to our family, Willie Easley, Richard James, Madison Easley, Michael Easley and Dawne Easley. We appreciate you for sharing in our dream and allowing us to work to make it a reality. We would also like to express our sincere appreciation to our friends and family who provided us with loving support, and kind words of encouragement along this journey, Elizabeth Williams, Gail Almond, Sophia Avery, Stephanie Pierce, Cheryl Daugherty, Cheryl Hill, Ron Evans, Lisa Rhymer, Brenda Annisette, Avis Hughley, Frances Reid Butler, Tiffany Ramirez, Daphne Bridges, Elayna Wilson, Tonya Sevier, Yolanda Sinkfield Thompkins, Linda Grays, Janet Hughes, Patricia Johnson, Ann Spurley, Gail Jones, Sherell Lee and Letra McCoy.

We thank you our editor, Denise Jones. Thank you to Candace Scott, our graphic designer, she is truly awesome and our web designers, Kevin and Shauna Easley, their work is phenomenal.

To all of the GEMMS who inspired us to help them reach their full potential, we love you. This book was born out of our desire to create GEMMS around the world. A special thanks to the public educators that believed in the GEMMS and shared our vision, Yvette Gunn, Barbara Gross, Sandra Williams, William Harding, and Dr. Inez Thomas. To our mentors who share in our passion for uplifting young people we say thank you. Your vision, dedication and commitment inspire us to keep, keeping on, Sandra Ervin, George Weathers and Dr. Mary Ann Hindes. No list of acknowledgements would be complete without mentioning the dynamic work and contributions of the GEMMS-maker, Dr. Sybil Mobley, past dean of Florida A&M University's School of Business and Industry.

We especially thank Dr. Matthew Johnson and his out-reach ministry for girls which enabled us to implement much of the material presented in this guide. We are grateful to Karen DeGannes, Esther Grissom, Arnetta Johnson, Kathy Roberson and the girls who participated in the ministry. We love you all very much.

We value the teachings and words of our pastor, Dr. Gerald Durley. His wise counsel and sound teaching have deeply impacted our mission and determination. We appreciate the love we receive from the Providence Missionary Baptist Church family.

A special thank you to those in the writing community that provided a positive word, Charisse Richardson, Shelia Moses, Curtis Bunn, the Sloans of the Southern Christian Writer's Conference and their distinguished faculty and the members of the Camp Creek Writer's Fellowship.

Finally, we thank all the girls around the globe, GEMMS in the making. Our Gifted, Elegant, Magnificent & Motivated Sisters – and the women who care enough to answer the call. We love you dearly. May God richly bless you!

ABOUT THE AUTHORS

Deana and Michelle Easley are a mother-daughter writing team. The inspiration to develop this guide was inspired by their work with girls groups in churches and schools. They are the founders of GEMMS: Gifted, Elegant, Magnificent & Motivated Sisters, a nonprofit organization.

Deana, mother of three and grandma of seven, is a retired public school educator with more than 32 years of classroom experience. Her goal has always been to ignite a passion for learning in each student she encountered. Mentoring young people became a natural extension of the classroom early in her career. As a foreign language teacher she used the classroom and study-travel trips abroad to expand the horizons of eager teen minds. She is a graduate of Clark-Atlanta University. When Deana is not writing she enjoys traveling, cooking, reading and mentoring her "grands".

Photograph by Michael Romeo

Michelle has dedicated her life to uplifting girls in urban communities. She received her Bachelor of Science degree in Business Administration and her Master of Business Administration degree from Florida A&M University's world renown School of Business and Industry. After graduating she spent several years in management at a fortune 500 company where she enjoyed an exciting career. After volunteering as a Project Business Consultant with Junior Achievement in St. Louis, Missouri, Michelle decided to answer the call and pursue a career in education full time. This led her to Emory University where she received a Master of Arts and Teaching degree. She began her career as an elementary school teacher in the public school system. Michelle spent several years in the classroom and then decided she would infuse students with her love of reading and books. She obtained a Specialist in Education degree from Georgia State University in Library Media Technology.

Michelle was the 2006 Braves/BellSouth Educator of the Year. She is a mother of two beautiful children, Richard and Madison. She is a native Atlantan. In her spare time she loves to read, listen to music, and travel. She is passionate about encouraging girls and young ladies to reach their full potential.

INDEX

NEED MORE COPIES

TITLE	PRICE	QUANTITY	TOTAL
THE MAKING OF GEMMS	$19.95	_____	_____

SUBTOTAL _____

SHIPPING _____
CONTINENTAL US PLEASE ADD $4.00 PER BOOK
OUTSIDE THE CONTINENTAL US PLEASE ADD $8.00 PER BOOK

TAX _____
GEORGIA RESIDENTS PLEASE ADD 7% SALES TAX

GRAND TOTAL _____

____ Money Order Enclosed

____ VISA, MasterCard (circle one)

Credit Card No. _____

Cardholder Signature _____

Expiration Date _____

SHIP TO:

PLEASE PRINT

Name (First) _____ (Last) _____

Address: _____Apt. No. _____

City _____ State _____ Zip _____

Phone _____ (include area code) Fax _____

Email address _____

I am interested in receiving a free e-newsletter each month. Yes _____ No _____

Positive Push Press, LLC
Post Office Box 43811
Atlanta, Georgia 30336
www.positivepushpress.com